IMAGE BY SILAS BATTON

BITE CLUB

THE OFFICIAL COOKBOOK OF THE BITE CLUB KITCHENS

By Chef Tony C.

Edited by H. J. Bigeck
and Sara Moritz

Printed in the United States of America.

First Printing, 2024

ISBN 979-8-9907994-1-7

www.biteclubnoms.com

DEDICATIONS

To my late Grandfather John, who inspired my love of cooking: I wish you knew how much you actually taught me, whether it be in the garage building patio furniture, replacing the hot water heater, or in the kitchen crafting a massive sandwich. I wouldn't be where I am today without your guidance when I was young. I can fix almost anything because you took the time to show me how. I really wish you were around today... I think you'd be proud of my kitchen... and my lawn.

To my late Grandmother Arline: where Grandpa taught me how to cook, you taught me how to bake and clean. The tricks you showed me on how to get stains out of cloths are still used to this day, which is extremely important in the kitchen! I really miss your cookies at Christmas time.

To Heather: you are the best co-pilot and a hell of a Sous Chef when I need you to be. You always take the reins and have my back at conventions and competitions, making sure I stay cool and collected throgh stressful times. When I start to feel overwhelmed, you remind me to "enhance your calm John Spartan" and that makes me smile and take a breath. You never question what is on the spoon when I shove it into your mouth, and you are one of the few people to honestly tell me when something I make tastes like shit... knowing you are not hurting my feelings, but helping me learn and grow. I love hearing you say, "great, now you've gone and ruined (insert mass produced food item here) for me because you make it better!"

To Flash and Methos: best damn cats a chef could ever have. I loved how you sat on a stool and watched me cook. I'd offer to let you smell and taste things while I explained what I was making. You helped me think things through, and calmed me down when I was stressed. Although you've both passed on, your paw prints are forever inked on my arm, to remind me to just keep being awesome-pawsome!

To all the fans of Bite Club:

YOU *are the reason we still are going strong today. Over the past 10 years, you've continued to share your excitement over the new stuff I've created, and I cannot thank you enough for your genuine support. Social media has let me down... but you, the fans, have followed the first Rule of Bite Club... you **TALKED** about Bite Club.*

I literally wish I could list everyone who's been a solid supporter, but I think this book would double in length. And every day I meet more and more people who love my creations. If it wasn't for Jody McQuarters and his Galaxy Art and Comic Con, and giving this scrappy nobody chef a table to present my products, I doubt Bite Club would be where it is today. Andrea, Jon, Bret, Bill, Wesley, Steve, Doc, Melissa, Donald, and Juan: you guys were all there on my first run and took me in as one of your own. You made me realise that art extends further then ink and paper, and I sincerely appreciate that. Nicole, you taught me the beauty of sourdough and made me see that the store-bought stuff is truly crap. Heather, Jess, Erin, and Liz, you were the inaugural class of Dames for Bite Club, and the roster has grown exponentially thanks to your leadership and example. Being surrounded by strong woman is empowering... plus you were never afraid to call me out on my bullshit.

I don't know what tomorrow holds, but I do know that right now I'm giddy and ecstatic. I'm just so happy to see Bite Club grow so much, and it's because of all of you.

I seriously love you all.

Chef Tony C.

"TREAT COOKING LIKE JAZZ, AND BAKING LIKE SCIENCE."

As you cook your way through this book, I'm sure you will find some recipes not up to your liking. Or you made them before from a much better recipe. Look up "Chicken Parmesan Recipe" on the internet... you'll find 100's of them, all slightly different. Statistically, you are not going to love every one. I'm not going to claim my recipes are the greatest. Taste is a funny thing, as in it's so unique to each person. Your grandmother's meatloaf is probably the greatest in the world, and no culinary god can make anything better than that. And that's awesome! I want to taste it! Invite me over! I'll bring the wine.

The recipes that follow are a collection of my favorites I've made many times over the years. They represent the passion I have in the kitchen. Some may rock your world. Others may leave you going "Meh". To the ones that leave you less than satisfied, I encourage you to experiment with them. Make them your own. Build upon them. Swap out ingredients. Add new flavors. That's how you learn in the kitchen. Every recipe ever written in history started off with "I wonder..."

But no matter what... have fun doing it.

Salaud!

CONTENTS

 See this symbol? This means a little cooking tidbit! These are scattered all throughout the book!

 Denotes when a recipe can be made vegetarian

WELCOME TO BITE CLUB

From the start, I've had trouble coming up with something to write for this part of the cookbook because it's difficult to convey what Bite Club is all about. Sure, in the broad sense, it's about food and recipes. But for me? Bite Club is a passion put into play and made public with an LLC and a WWW.

The first recipe written in here was transcribed from a scrap of an old cupcake box that I hastily wrote on in my grandmother's kitchen maybe 20 years ago. The ink is starting to fade and the edges along the torn part are softened from the constant movement in and out from my recipe bin every time I crafted it. This was from the original bullshit I had written here, more of a place holder then anything. Hell, I even had the generic Latin text filler that most publication programs have and thought I should just leave that in as a joke! It sounded smarter than anything I had written prior. I figured it would be the last thing I struggled to complete before it went off to print. I was right.

Putting what Bite Club is about into words is challenging, because Bite Club is me. And writing about myself has always been difficult. "Can you describe yourself in one word?" No. No one can.

Bite Club exists because I have a passion to create. I can't draw or paint, and musical prowess is non-existent. While I do have a bit of talent editing film and graphic design, my voice sucks for radio work.

So, I create with food.

Growing up in a very blue-collar family, I learned that food brought people together. No matter the schedules, dinner was always together. No TV, no phones, no toys, just the family. Parties in the backyard were a blast. There were coolers of beverages and tables laid out with food covered with those bug proof little tents... conversations were always between bites. Afterward, you were guaranteed to be sent home with a heaping plate of food. Christmas time would ensure a diabetic coma for days after. Mounds of cookies, cakes, nuts... this was all before the baked ham would come out of the oven!!!

I'd watch my Grandfather season the ribs, or my Grandmother roll out doughs. The food was never high end. Bologna and Spam were often fried and served up between Hostess bread... Hostess because one of their shipping stations was only three blocks from their house and they sold stuff fresh off the line for practically nothing. We're talking a loaf of Hostess white bread, bag still steamy, for 50¢. Remember the famous Hostess Ninja Turtle Pies??? 25¢ each! Cupcakes, Snoballs, you name it... thank god for my childhood metabolism!

Anyway, I quickly learned the importance of food. Not just food that tastes good... but food that was easy to make, could be made quickly, and doesn't need any crazy ingredients or special equipment. Comfort food. Family food. Call it what you will, it's what I grew up learning how to make. It's where my passion resides.

Bite Club has been and will always be about the everyday family. The busy Moms who need to put together a hearty, filling meal within an hour. The Dads who have to bring something to a school potluck. No crazy fancy ingredients, no super advanced cooking equipment. I've always said, if you can't find it at your local grocery store, you won't find it in this cookbook. Sorry if you were hoping for some Squid Ink Pasta or some dish that uses mushrooms only found on an acre of land on some island in the Pacific that's fertilized using poop from a sea turtle named Rodrigo and costs $180 an ounce. I believe the only "odd" ingredient in this book is filé powder for my Cajun dishes. Most supermarkets don't carry it, but it's easily found online.

When I started putting this book together, my goal was to make it as easy as possible to pull together a great meal using the tools most kitchens have. Everyone I know has at least one slow cooker (aka Crockpot), and most have a mixer. A grill may not be as common as those others, so I've made sure to include the oven method for those recipes. And ever since the electric pressure cooker craze from a few years ago, most have those somewhere in the kitchen. Some professional chefs call this "amateurish" or "cheating"...

I call it reality.

Whether you know your way around the kitchen very well or are just starting to transition from frozen meals to fresh, I hope this cook book aids you in becoming more confident in the kitchen. My grandfather once told me *"if you don't learn something new every day, consider the day wasted"*. I'd be giddy knowing one of my meals here made it into your dinner rotation.

I always tell people *"I never want to be **that** chef. I want to be **your** chef"*. I have no desire to go on cooking shows nor do I want my name on cookware. I just want to cook. And teach. And share. And feed. And cook more. I'm confident in what I do and I love doing it. I love doing it for everyone. I love playing with culinary science. I love cooking by my own rules. I love being challenged: tell me I can't do something, and I'll do it. And if I can't at first, I'll research the hell out of it, come back, and do it successfully... with my own twist on it. I love pissing off the naysayers. Like the great Sinatra once sang, "... I did it **MY** way." My way, for you.

So, I guess that's what I'm about... which means that's what Bite Club is about. Great food for the people, with a scoop of chaos theory, and a pinch of rebel attitude. Realistic cooking for the amazing everyday people out there. That's how I was taught to cook; that is how I will continue to cook.

WELCOME TO MY KITCHEN.

BEFORE WE START, LET'S TALK KITCHEN SAFETY.

Yeah yeah, I know... BORING! But I love you guys too much, so at least let me help you realize that some of the most basic things in the kitchen can turn on you in an instant.

You've probably heard the proverb *"An ounce of prevention is worth a pound of cure."* It means that it's easier to stop something from happening in the first place then to have to repair the damage after it's happened. And there is no other truer location for this advice then the kitchen.

HAVE A FIRE EXTINGUISHER THAT IS <u>MADE</u> FOR THE KITCHEN AND ALWAYS HAVE IT IN AN EASILY ACCESSIBLE LOCATION!

You can't dump water on a grease fire. Period. So, having an extinguisher specifically capable of handling kitchen fires is important. Check it every 6 months and buy it from a reputable manufacturer, they will last for years. Dropping 40 bucks now is nothing compared to what replacing your kitchen will cost.

KEEP YOUR KNIVES SHARP

Dull knives will do more damage than sharp ones. Sounds backwards, right? Ever try to cut a tomato with a dull knife? You put pressure on it, trying to break the skin, sawing with no progress, then SLIP! Knife slides off the tomato and all that force you were putting in it is transferred into the force of the blade, possibly coming down on your finger. Get a knife sharpening kit (or even those electric ones... better than nothing) and once every two weeks give your most used blades a once over.

KNIFE SAFETY

Besides keeping your blades sharp to reduce accidents, there are also a few general but extremely important rules to keep in mind about knives in and around the kitchen.

- If you are storing your knives in a kitchen drawer, invest in some kind of blade guards. These are durable plastic sleeves that slip over your knife blades. Not only will these keep your blades in great condition by protecting the edges from other things you throw in the drawer, but they also protect you if you blindly reach in for something.

- Always keep your dirty knives in plain view. If you toss them in a sink full of soapy water, it's really easy to forget about them and slice your hand open reaching in. Or someone else to reach in and hurt themselves. This also keeps the blades from getting damaged when you add other things to wash in the sink. *Keep your dirty knives in plain view until you are ready to wash them.*

- ***NEVER TRY TO CATCH A FALLING KNIFE!*** Professional kitchens have a saying: *"A falling knife has no handle".* Human nature is to try and catch something when we drop it (thank cell phones for that). Just let the knife fall while jumping back to ensure it doesn't impale your foot. I don't care if it's a cheap $20 blade or a $2000 custom santoku, a dinged or chipped blade is easier to deal with than stitches and nerve damage.

POTS AND LIDS

When cooking on the stovetop, always turn the handles of the pots so they are not sticking out from the stove. You have no idea how easy it is for that handle to catch a shirt and be pulled off the stove, splashing you, kids, pets, the cabinets, and appliances with hot stuff. As for lids, always lift lids away from you (meaning make sure the handle or knob of the lid faces you as you lift it). Steam burns are actually one of the most common kitchen accidents. Plus, things like thick sauces splatter while cooking, and you don't want hot pasta sauce in your eye.

GRAB IT RIGHT

Potholders and oven mitts have come a long way. From what was once basically a towel has evolved into fabric and material that can resist heat up to 2000°F. And keeping them in good condition is more important than you think. Make sure whatever kind you get/have fully cover your hand and wrist comfortably. Also, make sure they are easy to get on and off, yet loose enough to remove quickly if need be. If your cloth potholders look like they've handled molten lava, it's time to retire them. And once your silicone mitts have holes or rips, it will actually make things worse. If steam gets in there, your skin will stick to the wet silicone as it compresses and continues to burn you.

MAKE AN "OUCH POUCH" AND KEEP IT IN THE KITCHEN

Keep a secondary first aid kit made just for the kitchen. Contents: First aid cream, Silverdine or burn cream, wraps, gauze, Bleed Stop, and bandages of various sizes. I find liquid bandage is perfect for simple cuts on fingers, then covered with "finger condoms" for extra protection. Speaking of bandages...

... KIDS BANDAGES ARE THE BEST FOR THE KITCHEN!

You pop a bandage on a kid and what do they do? Run around outside. Get it SOAKED! Spill everything on it. Dig in dirt, playdough, and mud. And those things stay on. Regular bandages don't take to well to vinegars, oils, and fats. So suck it up, grab a box of those ninjitsu turtles, the wars in the stars, or the queens of that mouse corporation and feel safe knowing your freshly sharpened knife cut is going to stay covered.

ALWAYS HAVE CLEAR PATHWAYS WHILE COOKING

Make a plan when cooking certain foods. Boiling noods? Make sure the sink is empty and clear before you need to dump the water. All it takes is one bowl in the sink to rapidly change the direction of that boiling water! Going from stove to mixer? Make sure there's nothing spillable in the way and have absorbent materials in case of a spill. Pets, kids, or even a curled rug always seems to find your feet when you have something hot and splashy in your hands.

DRESS FOR SUCCESS

FEET: One thing I personally _always_ wear in my kitchens are "kitchen shoes". These are nothing special... usually either a retired regular pair of shoes or a pair of slip on breathable non-slip kitchen shoes. The point is I always have my feet covered. Why? Gravity is a bitch. Dropped utensils, splashed sauces, drips from spoons, shattered plates... they always head south. A basic shoe could make the difference between a major catastrophe and a simple accident.

ARMS: Ever reach into a hot oven and catch your forearm on the top? Enough said. I call these the "red badges of courage." If you look closely, my arms have a zebra pattern. At minimum, invest in oven mitts that are at least a foot long.

HAIR: Long hair should be tied up or back. Not only does it help keep it out of the food, but it also keeps it from catching in the equipment. You'd be shocked of how many stories I've heard of both men and women catching their hair in a mixer. And the only fix to that is slicing it off.

13

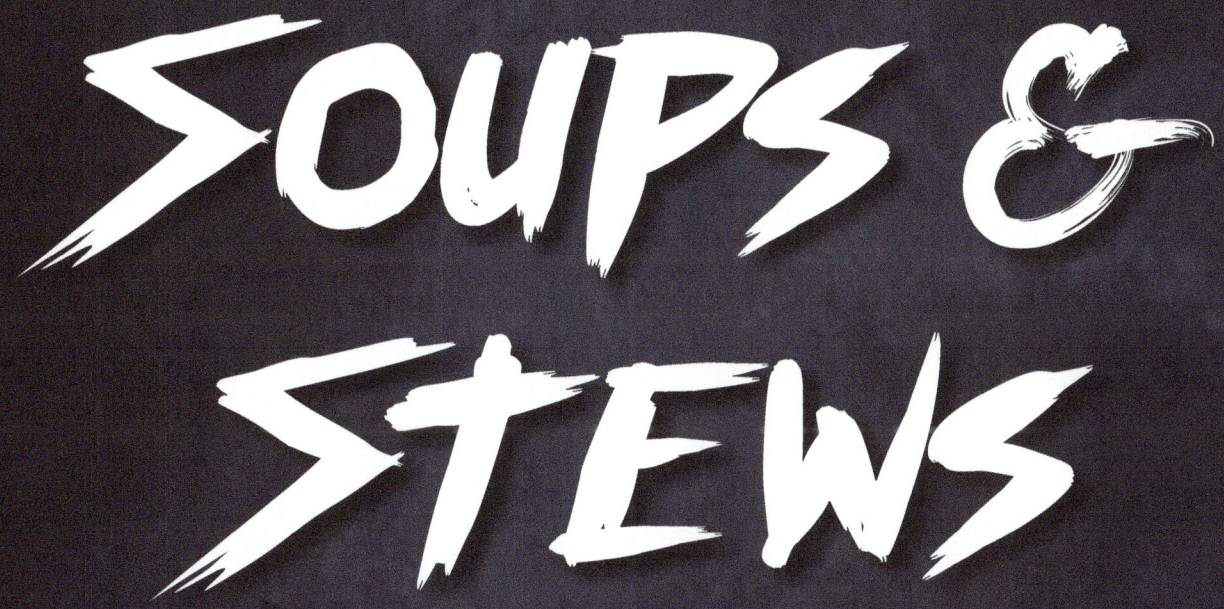

SOUPS & STEWS

"Only the pure of heart can make good soup."

- Ludwig Van Beethoven

"A first-rate soup is more creative then a second-rate painting."

- Abraham Maslow

"Almost every culture has its own variation on chicken soup, and rightly so - it's one of the most gratifying dishes on the face of the Earth."

- Yotam Ottolenghi

CREAMY CHICKEN & RICE

One could argue this is more of a "stew" then soup... and they'd be right! This was one of the first recipes I tackled as a young chef, making it over and over until I perfected it.

INGREDIENTS

- **2 Tablespoons butter**
- **1 Cup chopped onion**
- **1 Cup diced celery**
- **1 Cup diced carrots**
- **2 cloves garlic, minced**
- **4 Cups of chicken broth, homemade or canned.**
- **8 oz. of rice (your choice on kind, but strongly suggest wild rice)**
- **2 large boneless skinless chicken breasts diced into bite-size pieces**

- **1 teaspoon Kosher salt**
- **freshly ground black pepper to taste**
- **1 Tablespoon chopped parsley (or ½ Tablespoon dried)**
- **2 Tablespoons cornstarch**
- **2 Tablespoons water**
- **4 oz. cream cheese, cubed**
- **2 Cups milk (or 1 cup each of milk and half & half)**
- **splash of heavy cream**
- **1 Tablespoon lemon juice**

DIRECTIONS

Heat the butter in a large pot or dutch oven over medium high heat until shimmering. Add the onion, carrots, and celery and sauté for about 5 minutes, stirring occasionally until the vegetables are tender. Add the garlic, stir for 30 seconds. Stir in the chicken, chicken broth, rice, parsley, salt, and pepper.

Bring to a boil, then reduce heat and simmer for 30 minutes or until rice is tender and chicken is cooked through.

In a small bowl, whisk the cornstarch and cold water until smooth and add to the pot, stirring constantly. Raise the heat to medium high and stir in the cream cheese until melted. Stir in the milk, half-and-half, heavy cream, and lemon juice and cook until thickened. Serve sprinkled with more parsley if desired.

Unless you are on an incredibly strict and regimented doctor prescribed diet, NEVER omit the salt from the recipe.

Minestrone Soup

A simple soup, yet complex in flavors in textures. What's nice is this can come together in about 45 minutes from first chop to licking your chops. Don't be surprised if you enjoy this version better then that Italian chain.

Ingredients ✔

- 2 Tablespoons olive oil
- 2 medium carrots peeled, quartered, and sliced
- ½ onion, diced
- 1 zucchini, sliced into bite sized pieces
- 3 stalks celery, sliced
- 1 Tablespoon minced garlic
- 1 (14 oz.) can diced tomatoes
- 1 Tablespoon Italian seasoning
- 4 Tablespoons tomato paste
- 4 Cups vegetable broth

- ½ Cup cut green beans (frozen is fine)
- 1 (15 oz.) can cannellini beans, drained and rinsed
- 1 (15 oz.) can light red kidney beans, drained and rinsed
- 1 Cup small shaped pasta (like orzo, ditalini, stars, small shells, elbow farfalle, spirals, etc)
- 2 Cups spinach, stems removed
- 2 Tablespoons chopped fresh parsley
- ⅓ Cup finely grated parmesan cheese

Directions

Grab a large soup pot and heat the olive oil over medium heat. Toss in the celery, onion, carrots, and zucchini and cook until everything is tender, around 4-5 minutes. Once soft, pop in the garlic and cook for another 30 seconds.

Toss in the tomatoes (juice and all) and Italian seasoning. Cook for another minute to open up the seasoning flavor. Add the tomato paste, stir, and cook for another 2 minutes. Then add the broth and bring it to a simmer.

Once at a simmer, add all the beans and cook for 10 minutes. The pot should be at a nice simmer at this point, so add the pasta. Cook for another 8-10 minutes until the pasta is at your preferred tenderness.

Sprinkle in salt and pepper to taste. Drop in the spinach leaves and cook for 2-3 minutes or until they wilt.

Ladle into bowls, mugs, or the empty dreams of your enemies. Sprinkle the parmesan and parsley over the soup and enjoy.

"DETOX" SOUP

Detox teas, pills, powders, and the people who schlep these things on social media... it's all bullshit. Your body detoxifies itself. This soup isn't going to magically undo years of abuse from chemical rich fast foods... but it will be nourishing, healthy, and make you feel all warm and squishy inside.

INGREDIENTS

- **2 Tablespoons olive oil**
- **1 large onion, peeled and chopped**
- **2 Cups chopped celery**
- **3 Tablespoons fresh ginger, grated**
- **4 garlic cloves, minced**
- **1 ½ lbs. boneless skinless chicken breast, diced**
- **8 Cups chicken broth**
- **2 Cups sliced carrots**
- **2 Tablespoons apple cider vinegar**
- **¼ teaspoon crushed red pepper**
- **1 teaspoon ground turmeric**
- **3 Cups broccoli florets**
- **¼ Cup chopped flat parsley**
- **2 bay leaves**
- **Salt and pepper**

Slow Cooker

Toss everything but the broccoli into a slow cooker. Cover with broth and set to low for 8 hours, or high for 5 hours. Give that shit a stir every now and then... more to test the tenderness of the veggies. Add broccoli the last hour of cooking. Serve.

Pressure Cooker

Turn your 6-quart electric pressure cooker to the sauté setting and add the oil. Once hot, add the carrots, celery, and onion. Cook, stirring until the vegetables are slightly softened, 4 to 5 minutes. Add garlic during the last 30 seconds of sautéing. Cancel sauté setting.

Add all the other ingredients. Follow the manufacturer's guide for locking the lid. Set to pressure cook on high for 12 minutes.

After the pressure cook cycle is complete, quick release the pressure and wait until the cycle is complete. Be careful of any remaining steam, unlock, and remove the lid. Remove the bay leaves and discard. Season with salt and pepper and serve.

Stove Top

Set a large sauce pot over medium heat. Add the olive oil, chopped onions, celery, and carrots. Sauté for 5-6 minutes to soften. Add the ginger and garlic the last 30 seconds. Next, add the raw chicken breasts, broth, apple cider vinegar, red pepper, turmeric, bay leaves, and 1 teaspoon sea salt. Bring to a boil, lower the heat, and simmer for 20+ minutes until the chicken is cooked through.

Add the broccoli and parsley to the pot. Continue to simmer until broccoli has softened. Once the broccoli is tender, taste, then salt and pepper as needed. Serve.

To make this vegetarian, replace the broth with vegetable broth, and the chicken with diced portobello mushrooms.

ZUPPA TOSCANA SOUP

The true OG soup!

The thoughts of unlimited salad and breadsticks really gets those taste buds going huh? Bring that craving into your own kitchen and whip up a batch of this OG soup using better ingredients and a ton less salt! We also swap out the kale for fresh spinach for a more subtle and traditional flavor.

MAKE A BIG BATCH OF OUR QUICKY BREADSTICKS ON PG. 78 FOR YOUR OWN "UNLIMITED SOUP AND BREADSTICK" NIGHT!

INGREDIENTS

- 1 Tablespoon olive oil
- 1 lb. mild Italian sausage, casing removed
- 1 onion, diced
- 3 cloves garlic, minced
- 2 teaspoons dried oregano
- 6 Cups chicken broth
- 1 lb. russet or red potatoes, diced
- Kosher salt and freshly ground black pepper, to taste
- ½ bunch spinach, stems removed and leaves chopped
- 1 Cup half & half

Pressure Cooker

Set the pressure cooker to the sauté setting. Add olive oil and sausage. Cook, stirring frequently until sausage is lightly browned, about 3-5 minutes. Make sure to crumble the sausage as it cooks; drain excess fat.

Add onion and oregano. Cook, stirring frequently until onions have become translucent, about 2-3 minutes. Add garlic, cook for 30 seconds. Stir in potatoes and chicken broth; season with salt and pepper to taste.

Set to High Pressure and set time for 5 minutes. When finished cooking, quick-release pressure.

Kick the sauté setting back on and stir in spinach until wilted, about 1-2 minutes. Stir in half & half until heated through, about 1 minute; season with salt and pepper to taste. Cancel sauté setting. Serve and nosh!

Stovetop

Cook the Italian sausage in a pot over medium-high heat until crumbly, browned, and no longer pink, 10 to 15 minutes. Drain and set aside. Do not wipe the pot clean. That's gold on the bottom of the pan.

Cook the onions over medium high heat, about 5 minutes, until soft and translucent. Add garlic and oregano, cook for another minute.

Pour the chicken broth into the pot with the onion and garlic; bring to a boil over high heat. Add the potatoes and boil until fork tender, about 20 minutes. Reduce the heat to medium and stir in the half & half and the cooked sausage; heat through. Mix the spinach into the soup and cook till wilted, 1-2 minutes. Serve it up!

Mincing garlic? Rub some olive oil on your knife blade to keep it from sticking.

Need a salad to go with the OG Night? Toss some sliced tomatoes, thinly sliced red onions, pitted black olives, and croutons with the lettuce of your choice and whip up one of our vinaigrettes on page 26 to top it with!

CHICKEN STOCK

Once you make your own you'll never go back to store bought. Ok, you may, but I guarantee it won't be the same. This is a great weekend project, because you can make a large batch and freeze it. You can do this in a pressure cooker or a slow cooker, but to really let it rock is on the stove top over low heat for many, many hours.

INGREDIENTS

This will make about ½ gallon of stock. Feel free to double or even triple if needed, just make sure you have a pot big enough.

- 4 lbs. chicken bones (see notes below)
- 3 qt. cold water
- 4 oz. diced onion
- 2 oz. diced carrots
- 2 oz. diced celery
- 3 parsley stems
- 1 bay leaf
- 1 sprig of fresh thyme
- 1 Tablespoon of sea salt
- 1 Tablespoon of black peppercorns

Slow Cooker

Place all ingredients inside the slow cooker and fill with water until it is an inch from the top of the pot. Set to low and cook for a minimum of 8 hours, skimming occasionally. For deep, rich flavor, let it go for 24 hours! Strain stock and place in fridge. If you'd like a really clear stock, clean out strainer and place a coffee filter in, then strain the stock through that. Once cool, remove any fat that forms at the top. Use or freeze.

Stove Top

Rinse off the bones if you bought them fresh or frozen. Place the bones in the stock pot and cover with cold water. The water should be about 2 inches above the bones. Bring the pot slowly to a simmer. You are looking for what's known as a "bare simmer", where bubbles are breaking the surface infrequently.

Once you have the bare simmer going, skim the top of the liquid every 15 minutes. This will help produce a clear stock and remove the impurities that will cause spoilage. Simmer for 2 hours.

After 2 hours of simmering, add the onions, carrots, and celery (aka, the Mirepoix). Return the pot to a bare simmer and cook for 1 hour and 15 minutes.

Add the herbs, salt, and pepper and simmer for another 45 minutes.

Strain the stock and place it in the fridge to chill overnight. Skim any hardened fat from the top. The stock is now ready to be used or frozen.

Pressure Cooker

Place all ingredients into the pressure cooker and fill with water to max line. Lock in lid and pressure cook on high pressure for 90-120 minutes. Let pressure release naturally. Strain, chill, remove fat, then use or freeze.

Notes on bones: *Some meat left on the bones is okay. You know those roasted chickens supermarkets have? Those have PERFECT bones to create stock from. Buy one or two, enjoy the meat from it, pop the bones in a storage bag, and freeze it. When you have 2 or three of them, make stock!*

SAUCES

"An ounce of sauce covers a multitude of sins."

–Anthony Bourdain

"Woe to the cook whose sauce has no sting."

–Geoffrey Chaucer

BAJA SAUCE

What isn't this sauce great on??? Amazing on tacos, especially shrimp tacos. Great on a fish sandwich. Dip your fries or chips into it!

INGREDIENTS

- ¼ Cup sour cream
- ¼ Cup mayonnaise
- 1 teaspoon Old Bay
- ¼ teaspoon ground chili powder
- 1 ½ teaspoon finely chopped fresh cilantro
- 1 Tablespoon fresh lime juice
- OPTIONAL: splash of tequila

DIRECTIONS

Throw everything in a bowl. Mix it up! Cover and refrigerate for at least 1 hour. Adjust lime juice to achieve desired thickness.

AVOCADO SAUCE

You want to rock that Turkey Burger on pg. 55? Top it with a big spoonful of this!!!! Also good for anything wrapped up in a flour or corn shell.

INGREDIENTS

- ½ Cup sour cream (fat free is fine)
- 1 large ripe avocado, peeled
- 1 Tablespoon lime juice
- 2-3 Tablespoons minced fresh cilantro
- 1-2 garlic cloves, minced
- salt to taste

DIRECTIONS

Toss everything in a blender or food processor and rip it till smooth. Adjust consistency by adding more lime juice or sour cream to modify taste and thickness. Refrigerate until ready to use.

REMOULADE

There are a TON of remoulade recipes out there, but this has been our go to for years. It's simple and easy with common ingredients you most likely already have in the kitchen. Essential for a Cajun Style Po' Boy, this sauce can be made "hotter" by adjusting the amount of horseradish. Kick it up and clear out the sinuses! (You can find Ponzu in any Asian section of the market.)
Note: The base recipe as printed brings a sauce with flavor balance and a bit of heat.

INGREDIENTS

- ½ Cup mayonnaise
- 1-2 Tablespoons horseradish
- 2 Tablespoons lime Ponzu
- 1 teaspoon (dill) pickle relish
- 2 cloves garlic, finely minced
- ¼ teaspoon cayenne pepper
- dash of paprika
- 1 teaspoon Louisiana Hot Sauce (optional)

DIRECTIONS

MIX THAT SHIT UP!!!

TZAZIKI SAUCE

This sauce is known for gyros, but damnit if it isn't an amazing dip as well. Top the Turkey Burger (pg. 55) or the Black Bean Burger (pg. 56) with a heaping spoonful.

INGREDIENTS

- 2 medium English (or seedless) cucumbers
- 1 ½ Cups Greek yogurt (plain)
- 2 Tablespoons chopped fresh dill (or 1 Tablespoon dried dill)
- 1 ½ Tablespoons fresh lemon juice
- 1-2 cloves of garlic, minced
- ½ teaspoon Kosher salt
- 1 Tablespoon olive oil

DIRECTIONS

Grate the cucumber on a cheese grater (or if you have a food processor with a grating plate, use that!) Once grated, squeeze as much moisture out of it as you can. Don't worry about mushing the cucumber, you just want as much moisture out as possible. Once done, toss the cucumber and the rest of the ingredients into a bowl and mix together. It should be thick. Adjust salt for taste. For a stronger taste, you can add in a few sprigs of diced mint.

BC BURGER SAUCE

Traditional burger toppers like ketchup and mustard are fine... but sometimes you want a bit of zing for that burger. This sauce incorporates the classics, and brings in some acids to really cut through the fat and make the flavors shine!

INGREDIENTS

- ½ Cup mayonnaise
- 2 Tablespoons yellow mustard
- 1 Tablespoon dill relish
- 4 Tablespoons ketchup
- 1 teaspoon white vinegar
- ½ teaspoon garlic powder
- 2 teaspoons onion powder
- 1 teaspoon paprika

DIRECTIONS

Mix it all up and stash it in the fridge for at least an hour before usage.

TAPENADE SPREAD

Not really a sauce... but a necessity for our Muffuletta. Also works as a spread for a Charcuterie Board! And don't be put off by the anchovies in the traditional style. I promise you won't taste them at all, but they will add such a natural savory flavor.

TRADITIONAL STYLE

- 1 jar pitted Kalmata olives
- ¼ Cup good olive oil
- 2 anchovy fillets (rinsed) (or 1 teaspoon paste)
- 2 cloves of garlic
- 1 Tablespoon capers (drained)
- 1 Tablespoon lemon juice
- 3 fresh basil leaves
- dash of black pepper

Place all ingredients in a food processor and pulse till roughly chopped and blended.

BITE CLUB STYLE

- 1 can pitted black olives
- ¼ Cup olive oil
- 8 cloves of garlic
- 4 Tablespoons lemon juice
- ½ Cup fresh parsley
- 8 green onions, roughly chopped
- 1 Tablespoon chopped basil
- 2 Tablespoons parmesan cheese

Place all ingredients in a food processor and blend to a rough paste like consistency.

Red Onion Jam

Kick up those burgers, paninis, and bbq with this sweet, umami packed condiment. Slow browning the onions creates the Maillard reaction, in which sugars and amino acids break down and leads to a bunch of complex and wonderful flavors.

INGREDIENTS

- 3 large red onions, sliced
- 2 Tablespoons olive oil
- 1 Cup cheap red wine
- 3 Tablespoons honey
- 5 Tablespoons red wine vinegar
- 1 teaspoon each of salt and pepper

DIRECTIONS

Heat up the oil in a skillet on medium heat. Add onions, salt, and pepper. Cover the pan and cook for about 12-15 minutes until the onions are soft and reduced.

Crank the heat to high, add the wine, and simmer till the onions suck up most of the wine. Pour in the honey and red wine vinegar slowly and simmer, stirring occasionally until the onions become "jam-like", which will be in about another 15 minutes. Serve hot, cold, or best at room temp.

Bourbon Bacon Jam

INGREDIENTS

Bacon Jam is the ultimate condiment, bringing a sweet, savory, and amazing flavor to any sandwich, burger, or BBQ. It's a key ingredient for our Chulthor Burger on pg. 61, and makes for an incredible addition to any appetizer board!

- 1 lb. thick cut bacon, each slice quartered
- 2 extra large sweet onions, sliced thick
- ½ Cup brown sugar
- ½ Cup bourbon
- 1 Tablespoon balsamic vinegar
- 6 Tablespoons strong brewed coffee

DIRECTIONS

Cook the bacon over medium-high heat for around 10 minutes, stirring frequently until cooked but still chewy. A few crispy bits are ok. Use tongs to remove the bacon to a paper towel lined plate. Save 1 Tablespoon of the bacon grease. Sauté the onions in the reserved bacon grease for about 8-10 minutes, then reduce the heat to low. Stir in the brown sugar and continue cooking until the onions have caramelized, about 20 minutes. Increase heat to medium and add the bacon back in. Pour in the bourbon and coffee and continue to cook. Stir the mixture about every five minutes, for about 30 minutes. The consistency should be "jam-like". Remove from heat and stir in the balsamic vinegar. Use immediately or refrigerate for up to a week. Bring back to room temperature before serving. There will be little spots of white fat when you take it out of the fridge. As the jam comes to room temperature, these will disappear.

VINAIGRETTES

Don't stop these at salads! You can use vinaigrettes as a base for salsas and dips! Drizzle it over your meats or veggies towards the end of cooking. Use as a marinade for your proteins before cooking them! Or do what we do and brush them on breads before grilling or broiling!

PLACE ALL INGREDIENTS INTO A DRESSING SHAKER OR MASON JAR AND SHAKE SHAKE SHAKE!!!
All recipes are scalable. Go nuts! And we encourage you to experiment with spices and flavors!

BASIC VINAIGRETTE

- 3 Tablespoons olive oil
- 2 Tablespoons vinegar (any vinegar will work here and each will give you a unique flavor. Experiment!)
- salt & fresh-ground black pepper

OPTIONAL: Add 3 Tablespoons of sour cream to make this a Creamy Vinaigrette!

TANGY MUSTARD VINAIGRETTE

- 3 Tablespoons olive oil
- 2 Tablespoons red wine vinegar
- 1 teaspoon minced garlic
- ½ teaspoon Italian seasoning
- 1 teaspoon dijon mustard
- 1 Tablespoon honey

PEPPA & PARM VINAIGRETTE

- 3 Tablespoons olive oil
- 2 Tablespoons vinegar
- 3 Tablespoons sour cream
- 1 heaping Tablespoon grated parmesan
- pinch of salt
- ¼ teaspoon fresh ground pepper

STRAWBERRY FIELDS VINAIGRETTE

- 8 oz. frozen strawberries
- 3 Tablespoons apple cider vinegar
- 3 Tablespoons olive oil
- 2 Tablespoons honey
- ½ teaspoon salt & pepper

DIRECTIONS: Blend all ingredients till smooth.

ITALIAN VINAIGRETTE

- 3 Tablespoons olive oil
- 2 Tablespoons red wine vinegar
- 1 teaspoon minced garlic
- ½ teaspoon Italian seasoning

BALSAMIC VINAIGRETTE

- 3 Tablespoons olive oil
- 1 Tablespoon balsamic vinegar
- 1 teaspoon minced garlic
- ½ teaspoon Italian seasoning

WASABI VINAIGRETTE

- ¾ Cup olive oil
- ¼ Cup rice vinegar or rice wine vinegar
- ¼ Cup soy sauce
- 2 teaspoons wasabi paste
- Salt and pepper to taste

CILANTRO-LIME VINAIGRETTE

- 2 Cups fresh cilantro
- ¼ Cup fresh lime juice (2-3 limes)
- 2 teaspoons honey
- 1 garlic clove
- 1 teaspoon lime zest
- ½ teaspoon Kosher salt
- ½ teaspoon ground coriander
- ½ Cup extra-virgin olive oil
- ¼ Cup vinegar

OPTIONAL: Add 1 avocado or ½ Cup Greek yogurt to make this a creamy delight!

DIRECTIONS: In a food processor, place all ingredients except oil and pulse till smooth. With the blade running, stream in the olive oil and blend until incorporated.

DRESSINGS

Place all ingredients in a food processor or blender and blend to desired consistency.

WASAB-ACADO DRESSING

- ½ avocado
- ½ Tablespoon wasabi paste
- 1 lime, juiced
- 1 teaspoon sesame oil
- 1 ½ Tablespoons rice wine vinegar
- 1 Tablespoon pickled ginger

(If too thick, thin with equal amounts of lime juice and rice wine vinegar)

CREAMY CILANTRO DRESSING

- ½ Cup mayo
- ½ Cup packed fresh cilantro
- ¼ Cup buttermilk
- 2 Tablespoons chopped green onion
- 2 Tablespoons apple cider vinegar
- ½ teaspoon salt
- ¼ teaspoon black pepper

(If too thick, thin with equal amounts of buttermilk and apple cider vinegar)

GINGER-LIME DRESSING

- ¼ Cup fresh lime juice
- 2 Tablespoons rice vinegar
- 1 Tablespoon low sodium soy sauce
- 1 Tablespoon fresh grated ginger
- 2 teaspoons sugar
- 1 Tablespoon finely diced green onion
- 2 Tablespoons canola or vegetable oil
- Salt to taste

(If too thick, thin with equal amounts of soy sauce and rice vinegar)

LEMON TAHINI DRESSING

- ¼ Cup tahini
- 3 Tablespoons cold water
- ½ teaspoon minced garlic
- ¼ teaspoon Kosher salt
- 5 Tablespoons lemon juice
- ½ teaspoon cumin

(If too thick, thin with equal amounts of lemon juice and water)

POPPIN' SEED DRESSING

- 1 ½ Tablespoons sour cream
- 1 ½ Tablespoons apple cider vinegar
- 1 Tablespoon milk
- 2 Tablespoons sugar
- ¼ Cup mayo
- 1 ½ teaspoons poppy seeds

(If too thick, thin with equal amounts of milk and apple cider vinegar)

CLASSIC ITALIAN DRESSING

- ¼ Cup white wine vinegar
- ½ Cup olive oil
- 1 Tablespoon honey
- 1 Tablespoon lemon juice
- 4 Tablespoons parmesan
- 1 teaspoon onion powder
- 1 ½ teaspoons dried oregano
- 1 teaspoon dried basil
- 1 teaspoon dried parsley
- 2 teaspoons garlic powder
- ¾ teaspoon salt
- ½ teaspoon pepper

You can add ½ Cup mayo to this to make it a creamy dressing!!!

Say it with me... THERE IS NO SUCH THING AS TOO MUCH GARLIC!

Pasta Sauce

This pasta sauce is a fusion of my grandparent's recipe with some modern culinary science. This is another dish where the more time it goes for, the better it gets. I've been known to let this cook for 12-18 hours. But I know some of you won't have all day to dedicate to it, so we've included a "quick version" that skips the roasting and uses your favorite canned tomatoes, relying on the fresh ingredients to punch up that flavor.

Roasted Version

- 3 Tablespoons olive oil
- 3 lbs. ripe small to medium sized tomatoes (see notes), cut in half
- 1 large head of garlic, peeled and each clove halved
- 1 medium onion or 3 shallots, cut into 8ths
- 2 Tablespoons fresh oregano (or 1 Tablespoon dried)
- 2 Tablespoons fresh basil, torn (or 1 Tablespoon dried)
- 2-3 springs of fresh thyme (or 2 teaspoons dried)
- 2 teaspoons Kosher salt
- 1 teaspoon sugar (optional, see rant on pg. 28)
- 1 ½ lbs. crumbled and cooked meat (ground beef, Italian sausage, prosciutto, pancetta)
- splash of soy sauce

Notes

You can use any kind of tomato, just keep in mind that larger tomatoes may require you to remove the seeds and core, and will produce more juice when roasting. Plum, Roma, or Cocktail tomatoes are almost perfect, as they do not give off a lot of liquid and will skin easily after roasting.

✔ To make this vegetarian, replace the meat with mushrooms, thinly sliced carrots, bell peppers, cubed squash, sliced and drained zucchini… or a mix of these! Roast with tomatoes.

Directions

Get that oven rockin' to 400°F. If you have a convection oven, set it to convection roast! Brush a sheet tray with a bit of olive oil. Sprinkle the herbs down first. Then place the tomatoes, cut side down, over the herbs. Next, toss in the garlic and onion or shallots between the tomatoes. Drizzle the rest of the olive oil over everything.

Pop the sheet pan in the oven and roast for about 30 minutes. If you are using larger tomatoes it may take an additional 10 minutes. You want the skins of the tomatoes starting to blister and peel off.

Remove from the oven and let cool slightly. You should be able to just grab the skins of the tomatoes and pull them off with minimal effort. Dump everything (juices included) into a large pot on the stove top. Smash everything with a potato masher or immersion blender. If you do not have any of these toys, place all ingredients in a blender, pulse a few times, then dump into a pot on the stove top.

Season with salt and pepper. Add the cooked meats, give a good stir, cover, and simmer. At this point the sauce is ready to go, but the longer you let it simmer, the deeper the flavor develops. Cover and simmer for 8 hours over low heat, stirring about every 30 minutes. If it's too thick, add in beef broth, ½ Cup at a time and stir to combine. Taste. Add sugar, ½ teaspoon at a time, till your desired flavor emerges. Splash the pot with soy sauce and stir before serving.

STOVETOP "QUICK" VERSION

- 1 lb. lean ground beef
- 1 lb. Italian sausage (casing removed if needed)
- ½ sweet onion, diced
- 5 cloves garlic, minced
- 1 (28 oz.) can crushed tomatoes
- 12 oz. plain tomato sauce
- 1 (6 oz.) can tomato paste
- ½ Cup beef stock or broth
- 2 teaspoons dried basil
- 1 teaspoon Italian seasoning
- 1 teaspoon salt
- ½ teaspoon pepper
- splash of soy sauce

DIRECTIONS

Grab a large pot and pop that on top of the stove over medium heat. Drizzle in a bit of olive oil and brown the ground beef and sausage. Once the fat starts rendering out, toss in the diced onion and cook till the meat is browned and the onions start becoming translucent. Dump in the garlic and cook for a minute. Remove the contents into a fine mesh strainer to release most of the fat and excess moisture. DO NOT WIPE OUT POT. Add the beef, sausage, onions, and garlic back into the pot and stir in the remaining ingredients.

Reduce heat to low and cover. Stir every 30 minutes. Taste after an hour of simmering. Add in additional salt/seasonings to your liking. Simmer for an additional hour. Taste again and adjust. If too acidic, sprinkle in a bit of sugar (see rant on next page about this). 5 minutes before serving, splash in a bit of soy sauce and stir.

NOTE: You can cook this for longer than 2+ hours to really meld and pop flavors. If you find the sauce too watery, offset the lid to let the steam escape. If too thick, stir in a bit more beef broth and tomato paste.

SLOW COOKER VERSION

Perfect to set it in the morning and just let it go while the day passes on, ready when everyone gets home. You can actually precook the meats and onions the night before, and mix everything together in the crock of the slow cooker. Store in fridge overnight, then in the morning pop the crock into the slow cooker housing and set the temp. If you do this, just add an hour to the cooking time to adjust for the cold ingredients.

DIRECTIONS

Follow ingredients above. Cook meats and onions in pan on stovetop, then dump into strainer. Pour meats, onions, and remaining ingredients into crock of slow cooker, then cook on low for 7-9 hours or on high for 4-5 hours. If sauce is too thin offset the lid the last 2 hours of cooking (low) or last hour (high).

STOP adding oil to your pasta water! It hurts more than anything. It doesn't keep your noodles from sticking together, because oil floats on the surface while noodles sink (constant stirring and proper water to noodle ratio keeps them from sticking). Plus as you remove the noodles to strain them, the oil THEN clings to the noods, preventing your sauce from adhering.

SUGAR IN SAUCE = PINEAPPLE ON PIZZA
How's the weather up there on your high horse?

Back in the summer of 2022, a friend posted an innocent question on social media. They asked, "Do you add sugar to your homemade pasta sauce?" The answers came in, some simply "yes" or "no", others were strongly worded, as in "Fuck No!"

I answered "Yes*" (the asterisk included). Since my social media handles all contain the word "Chef" in them, this often leaves me open for either attacks or direct questions. The sugar in the sauce question and my answer seemed to draw ire from one particular person, who instantly went into attack mode and stated that my "Nana would die of disappointment". Ok then. I checked out their profile, and they had chef as a "job" but not where (usually means home cook).

I replied to their comment with "Why would Nana die over a teaspoon of sugar?" They went on to say that San Marzano tomatoes are sweet enough, adding sugar to your sauce is just covering up a shitty sauce, and only amateurs put sugar in their sauce.

Normally I'd go into attack mode, but I've been trying to curb my quick reaction and think calmly first before destroying someone. I took a deep breath and asked if they lived in an area where San Marzano tomatoes are grown and can get them fresh. They said no, that they use canned.

I responded "That's great. You use whatever works for you. On your profile, you state you are a chef... yet you immediately jump to attack something you have an opinion about rather than inquire why, like a 'true' chef would. So I'll just go ahead and answer the question you never asked. While you prefer to support a faceless corporation using canned tomatoes because they are all the rage right now, I prefer to support my local farmers and craft something amazing with their goods. And here in the Midwest, our soil doesn't produce a sweet tomato, so we have to adjust for the acidity. If a scant teaspoon of raw cane sugar per pound of tomatoes puts me on some exiled list, so be it. But if the popularity of my pasta sauce from the numerous successful pop-ups, awards, and private dinners is any indication... it seems people don't mind a bit of sugar to balance their local produce. I think your Nana would be more disappointed in your canned tomatoes and not fresh."

They never replied. My response racked up dozens of reactions, all positive.

The term "To Each Their Own" comes to mind here. You do you. Want to make sauce from cans? Go for it. Fresh? Awesome. Want to open a jar and dump it on pasta? Whatever makes you happy. I've made sauces with canned San Marzano tomatoes before, where I agree with the troll "chef" that sugar was not needed, thus the * in my response to the original question. It's a batch by batch decision, as all cooking is.

The whole pineapple on pizza is the poster child for this debate. I have actually read comments by people that threatened literal harm on someone for putting pineapple on pizza. Unfortunately, this has become the norm. Our opinions are the be-all-end-all and anything that goes against it is instantly wrong.

And sadly, this has stretched over everything. From games (Xbox vs. Playstation vs. Nintendo), to vehicles, pets (dog owners vs. cat owners), music, artist, and especially politics. "If you don't like/believe/support/buy what I do, you are a piece of shit and should just die." And I've seen it from both sides. "Oh, you DON'T put pineapple on your pizza?!? Well you are just a closed-minded fuck and should die!"

Want to know something funny? The people who are strongly anti-pineapple on pizza… have probably never even tried it. They just hopped on the social bandwagon to hate for the sake of hating. I've said it early on in this book… taste is far from universal. Me? Pineapple on pizza isn't bad. The acid from the fruit slices through the savory of the cheese and dough. It's not my personal go-to pizza order, but I wouldn't spit in my friend's eye and burn down their house if they made it for dinner one night. Born and raised in Chicago, I have pretty strong feelings for pizza (and I don't care if you put ketchup on your hotdog! Yeah, I said it, come at me!). But New York pizza is pretty damn good. Not a fan of Detroit style… but one of my best friends LOVES it. Awesome! Enjoy. When spending a bit of time in Oklahoma and watching people put ranch on pizza, I'll admit it made my eye twitch a bit at first, because ranch plus pizza is too much for the tongue to handle (it's a sensory overload for the brain and tongue… more on that later in the book).

Instead of attacking someone because their food/cooking methods/taste is different then you, try asking "why?" Why do you add the sugar? Why the splash of soy sauce? What is it about the pineapple on the pizza that you enjoy?

You just might learn something new rather than spew more hate on an already toxic platform.

BITE CLUB'S ITALIAN BREAD

Crusty, Fluffy, Universal Perfection

This is a great base bread recipe that's perfect for making rolls, buns, boules, bread bowls, and even breadsticks if you desire! Easily customizable with herbs or seasonings. Double the recipe if need be. The base will give you 2 personal sized boules.

INGREDIENTS

- 1 ½ Cups warm water (100-110°F F)
- ½ teaspoon white sugar
- 1 Tablespoon (or 1 packet) active dry yeast
- ½ Tablespoon salt
- 2 Cups of bread flour
- 1 ½ Cups all-purpose flour

(You can use all bread flour or all AP flour for this. See below for the difference in results.)

Get your water to the recommended temperature range. Use a damn thermometer, don't "feel test" it. Our hands usually run hotter or colder, so it's hard to be precise. You know why? Too hot and you kill the yeast. Like I said before... "Treat cooking like jazz and baking like science."

Measure out your water and add in the yeast and sugar. Give it a quick stir and let it sit for about 10 minutes. It should be foamy with a good head bubbling after the time. If not, your yeast is probably too old... or you "feel tested" the water and killed the yeast. I warned you.

Dump in 2 ½ Cups of the flour and mix (low speed if using a mixer with a dough hook) till smooth. If still kinda moist, add in the remaining flour, ½ Cup at a time. Once the dough is smooth, cover with a towel and let rest for 20 minutes. While resting, boil a small pot of water and pop the light in the oven on.

After 20 minutes, mix in the salt and the rest of the flour (and any herbs or seasonings you wish), and continue kneading/mixing till the dough is soft and smooth. Spray a clean bowl with baking spray, toss the dough in, and cover with a clean dish towel. Place the bowl in the oven with the pot of boiling water. Close the oven and don't open it until the dough has at least doubled in size. The oven light plus boiling water makes for a perfect makeshift steam proofing cabinet.

Once doubled, remove from the oven and punch it down. Cover and place back into the oven. Let rise until doubled again. Remove and punch down again. Turn off the oven light, remove pot of water, and preheat the oven to 450°F. While oven is preheating, cut and shape dough. Place dough on silicone lined cookie sheets, place cookie sheets on top of oven, cover with a towel and let rise again.

Once risen, score top of loaves with sharp knife, mist with water, place in oven, and bake till golden brown and sounds hollow when tapped on. (Times will vary depending on shape. Start checking around 10 minutes.)

BREAD FLOUR vs. ALL PURPOSE FLOUR

Bread flour has a higher protein content *(12-14%)*, resulting in a chewier final product with more structure *(aka fluffiness)*. It's perfect for breads, pizza dough, breadsticks, fluffy fried donuts, pretzels, etc. All purpose flour has a lower protein content *(9-12%)*, which will give you a more tender final product, like cakes, cupcakes, muffins, pie crusts, biscuits, etc.

SANDWICHES

Grinder   poor Boy   Blimpie

HERO   Hoagie   SUB

Sammie   WEDGE   Dagwood

A sandwich can be anything you want... any filling, any bread. Your imagination is the limit. But it's also an art. Meat to bread ratio, wet and dry ingredient stacking, types of spreads... Most of the time it'll be good. Sometimes it'll be shit. And sometimes it'll be the greatest thing you've ever crammed in your maw.

Let's aim for the latter...

PULLED PORK

Our pulled pork pops up in a few recipes in this book, so it's fitting we start here. I've had a lot of questions in the past about the kind of pork to use. Traditionally, pork shoulder or pork butt (not the actual pigs butt... you ass) are used, but it can be made with pork loin. Pork shoulder/butt will result in a moist shredded pork due to the higher fat content, whereas pork loin will be a bit on the dryer side when shredded. Not a bad thing by far, and each have their benefits. You can moisten up pulled pork loin just by reintroducing some of its liquid after shredding. Plus, if you are just cooking for one or two, it's easier to get a 1 lb. loin vs. a 5 lb. shoulder.

Slow Cooker Method

- **2-4 lbs. pork shoulder/butt/loin**
- **1 Cup rub (next page)**
- **2 liters of Cherry Dr. Pepper or root beer**

Cover pork with rub and massage in for about a minute, getting into all the cracks and crevices of the meat. Get intimate with it! Stop making it weird!

Heat a pan on the stovetop and sear the pork, 3-4 minutes per side. Then place in slow cooker. Pour the soda around the meat (do not pour on top, you want that rub to sit) until the meat is about ¾ covered (you probably will not need the entire 2 liter). Pop the lid on and set it to low for 8-10 hours or high for 5-6 hours.

Remove pork from slow cooker (careful, it WILL fall apart) and shred the pork using 2 forks or meat claws. Dump the liquid from the slow cooker and return the shredded meat to the cooker to keep warm.

NOTE: If using a pork loin, reserve 1 Cup of the cooking liquid before draining. Once meat is returned to the slow cooker after shredding, pour in the reserved liquid and mix it with the pork. You may not need all the liquid. Alternatively, you can forgo the reserved liquid and just pour in the bbq sauce of your choice.

Pressure Cooker Method

- **4 lbs. pork butt roast, boneless or bone-in/loin**
- **2 Tablespoons olive oil**
- **⅓ Cup rub (see next page)**
- **1 ½ Cups Cherry Dr. Pepper or root beer**
- **1 Tablespoon Worcestershire sauce**
- **2 teaspoons liquid smoke**

Trim fat from the pork and cut into 4 equal sized cubes.

Add 2 Tablespoons oil to pressure cooker and set to sauté. Once ready, place 2 pieces of the pork and sear on each side for about 2 minutes each. Remove pork and repeat with remaining pork pieces.

Once pork is seared and removed from pot, press cancel and add 1/2 Cup of the soda. Use a wooden spoon and scrape the bottom of the pot (those "burnt" bits are pure flavor). Add remaining liquid, Worcestershire, and liquid smoke.

Place pork directly into the liquid in the pot, giving a bit of room for each chunk. Secure lid and make sure vent is set to sealing. Pressure cook/manual on high pressure for 60 minutes. Natural pressure release until the pin drops. Remove pork to cutting board and shred with 2 forks or meat claws. Dump liquid from pot (reserving 1 Cup if making pork loin). After shredding, return pork to pot and pour in BBQ sauce or some of the reserved liquid (not all at once) and toss pork.

For a perfect sear on meats, pat it completely dry before placing it in a super-heated pan.

PULLED CHICKEN??

Replace soda with chicken broth/stock. Follow the same cooking directions as above, except only pressure cook for 15 minutes, with a 10-minute natural release. Lastly, you only need to reserve ½ Cup of the liquid.

Oven Roasting Method

- **4 lbs. boneless pork shoulder**
- **2 Tablespoons vegetable oil**
- **rub or spices of your choice**
- **12 oz. lager/broth/soda/beer**

Preheat oven to 300°F. Trim excess fat from pork and cut into large pieces to fit in a large Dutch oven. Massage in spices/rub.

Place Dutch oven over medium high heat and pour in oil. Working in batches, add pork and sear on all sides. Watch for burning, as spices can burn quickly.

Once pork pieces are seared on all sides, pour liquid around pork and cover with lid. Pop the Dutch oven into the oven and cook until pork is beginning to turn tender, about 3 hours. Remove lid and cook for another 1-2 hours. Depending on your oven, more or less time may be needed. Insert a fork into the pork and slightly pull... does it start to shred easily? Then it's ready

Remove pork from Dutch oven and let rest, 15-20 minutes.

Shred pork using two forks or badass meat claws.

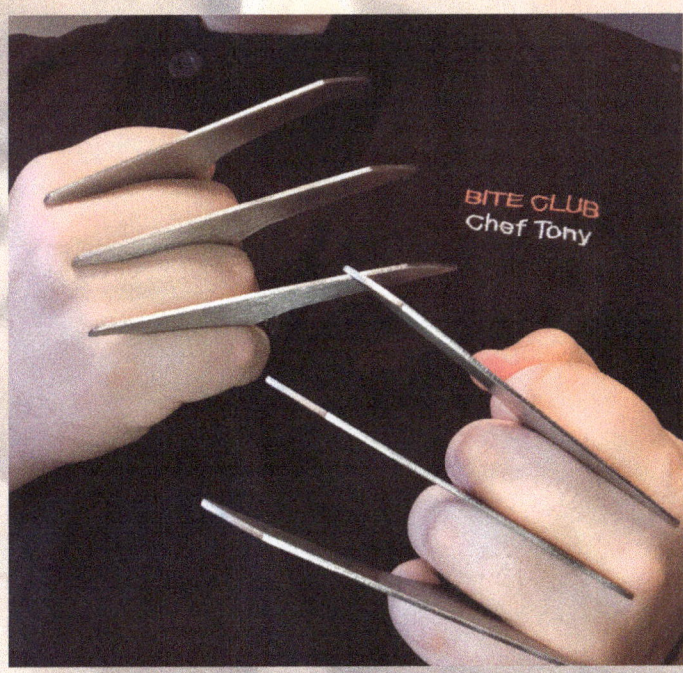

MEAT CLAWS!!!

Basic Rub Recipe

This rub recipe is a great starting point. Use it as is or start adding in different spices to create your own unique blend.

- **½ Cup brown sugar**
- **4 Tablespoons paprika**
- **2 Tablespoons Kosher salt**
- **1 Tablespoon pepper**
- **1 Tablespoon garlic powder**
- **1 Tablespoon onion powder**
- **1 Tablespoon chili powder**
- **(Optional) 1 teaspoon red pepper**

Toss all into a mason jar or bowl with tight fitting lid and shake the hell out of it to mix thoroughly. Break up brown sugar clumps with a fork or small whisk. Will keep for many months if sealed tightly.

THE CUBANO

This is by far my favorite sandwich to nosh.

How do you go wrong with pulled pork, cheese, pickles, and ham with a rich mustard? You can't!!! The savory elements are brought to life by the acids from the mustard and pickles. Normally, this is made with Cuban bread, so if you can find/make it, awesome. However, a crusty French or Italian loaf will work just as good.

INGREDIENTS

- crusty French, Italian, or Cuban loaf
- Pulled Pork (pg. 34)
- Dijon or yellow mustard
- pickle slices
- deli ham, sliced thin.
- Swiss cheese

HEY, WHY NO INGREDIENT AMOUNTS???

This is one of those magical recipes where YOU decide how much to make. Since you already made the Pulled Pork from pg. 34, everything else is already done. Pile on the pork, use more or less cheese, or make it Chef Tony style and pickle the Hell out of that sammich!

DIRECTIONS

Assemble the sandwich by splitting the bread in half, coating each half in mustard, then layering the ingredients in this order: cheese, pickles, ham, pork, and another layer of cheese, then top with mustard smeared bread half. When you heat this sandwich up, the cheese glues everything together.

PANINI PRESS: Heat up the press, place the sandwich inside, and close press. Apply pressure to the press to flatten the sandwich as much as possible.

STOVETOP: Brush the outside of assembled sandwich with a light layer of melted butter. Heat up 2 similar sized pans on the stove top over medium heat (cast iron would be great but not needed). Place the sandwich in one pan and place the second preheated pan on top of the sandwich. Cook 5-7 minutes per side while applying pressure to the top pan. Cooking times may vary greatly.

OVEN: Preheat oven to 425°F. Brush the outside of assembled sandwich with a light layer of melted butter and wrap tightly in foil. Place on a baking sheet and stack another baking sheet on top with a heavy ovenproof pan or a pizza stone. Bake for about 20 minutes, remove, and nosh.

Don't get discouraged if you are trying to replicate a dish you had at a restaurant and you just can't get the flavor to match. The difference between their recipe and yours? About 4x the butter, salt, and added flavor enhancers.

THE PORKANATOR

Hasta La Vista, Diet!

I developed this after being told by a sandwich shop to "fuck off" when asked about their pork cooking methods, because it seemed really "rubbery". So, I said "Ok" and vowed to make a bigger, better version of their sandwich. I guess when you use frozen bulk shredded pork and uber mass produced cheese, you'd get a bit testy too when asked about it. Their shop doesn't exist anymore, but my version does.

INGREDIENTS

- **crusty French loaf, Italian loaf, or your favorite thick "go-to" buns**
- **melted butter (about 2 Tablespoons)**
- **Pulled Pork (pg. 34)**
- **BBQ sauce**
- **provolone cheese slices**
- **cooked strips of thick bacon**
- **thick deli sliced ham**

DIRECTIONS

This is another sandwich where YOU decide the amounts. But the trick is not over stuffing the bread, because although you are building it "open face" style, you are eventually going to have to close this monstrosity!

Kick on the broiler in the oven. Slice each of the loves lengthwise (but don't cut all the way through. You want to leave a bit for a hinge). Open the bread up and brush with the melted butter. Place the bread on a sheet pan and place under the broiler. Be careful, you don't want to burn it. You just want it toasted. This is important to keep the bread from going soggy.

Heat up a pan on the stove top and cook up the ham. You just need it warmed. Once the bread is toasted, layer on the thick slices of ham on each side, then a couple slices of cheese, followed by the pulled pork, and finally the bacon, but limit it to one side. Place back on the sheet pan and place back under the broiler. Cook for 3-4 minutes until the cheese starts to melt under the pork. Remove from broiler. This also will crisp up the ends of the pulled pork nicely.

Slather on your favorite bbq sauce and close the beast up. Unhinge your jaw like a snake to enjoy this monster.

Po' Boys

New Orleans Classic, Bite Club Style!

There are a million different recipes out there for a Po' Boy. From different batters for the meat to what gets put inside... and that's just the sandwich part! The remoulade has another million different versions! We keep it simple and easy for you without sacrificing the authentic NOLA flavors! Serve this up with some Beignets (pg. 110), Gumbo (pg. 97), or Jambalaya (pg. 96).

INGREDIENTS

- **vegetable oil for deep-frying**
- **4 French rolls**
- **4 Tablespoons melted butter**
- **2 teaspoons minced garlic (or 1 teaspoon garlic powder)**
- **3 eggs, beaten**
- **hot sauce**
- **¾ Cup all-purpose flour**
- **¼ Cup corn starch**
- **2 Tablespoons Creole seasoning**
- **2 lbs. jumbo shrimp, peeled, and tails removed**
- **2 Cups panko bread crumbs**
- **shredded lettuce**
- **Remoulade (from pg. 23)**

DIRECTIONS

Turn on oven broiler. Combine butter and garlic and spread on rolls. Toast in broiler until golden brown.

Heat oil in a 2-quart saucepan to 375°F. Mix together the Creole seasoning, corn starch, and flour.

Whisk the eggs with a few dashes of hot sauce. Dredge the shrimp in flour, then egg, then press in the panko. Fry the coated shrimp in batches until golden brown and remove to a paper towel lined plate or sheet pan.

Spread remoulade on all halves of the rolls. Top with shrimp, followed by shredded lettuce.

NOTES

Although we have shrimp listed, this sandwich can be filled with any other classic Bijou proteins. Try replacing the meat with fried crawfish. Or fried clams. Even chicken will work! And if you can get your hands on it, farm raised alligator is freaking amazing deep fried and piled high. A dedicated butcher can most likely get you some. It'll be a bit pricy but live a little and give it a try! You won't be sorry.

SRIRACHA JOE'S

Let's Kick up a Cafeteria Classic!

Don't lie... you freaking love a good sloppy joe. Memories of grade school or Billy Madison come flooding back at the mere thought of these. By incorporating sriracha, we bring out a new depth of flavors with a bit of heat. Spoon the meat onto the bun, top with potato chips, and smash it down for the ultimate flashback food! And use any ground protein you like! Beef, turkey, chicken, buffalo, ostrich, dinosaur... just don't use ground sausage..

INGREDIENTS

- 1 lb. lean ground beef or other ground protein
- 1 Tablespoon olive oil
- ¼ Cup fine diced onion
- ¼ Cup diced green pepper
- 1 teaspoon garlic powder
- ½ Cup ketchup
- 1 teaspoon yellow mustard

- ¼ Cup sriracha (or if you have Gochujang, you can use that) *SEE NOTES
- 1 Tablespoon + 1 teaspoon brown sugar
- salt and pepper
- BUNS FOR SERVING

DIRECTIONS

Over medium heat, heat up olive oil, then add onion and green peppers. After 2 minutes, add in ground beef and cook till brown. Pour into strainer to allow most liquids to drip out, then return mixture to skillet.

Stir in remaining ingredients and mix thoroughly. Reduce heat and simmer for 30 minutes or until desired thickness is achieved.

NOTES

You can add more sriracha but you will have to simmer it longer to thicken. Also, sriracha has a good amount of salt in it, so adjust accordingly.

Also, try slapping some hamburger dills on this... the acid of the vinegar cuts through the natural umami of the beef and ketchup for a balanced and kick ass flavor!

MUFFELETTA

Bigger than your head and tastier then your dreams.

This is basically an Italian charcuterie board dumped into a gutted round bread boule. If you want to make your own, give our Italian Bread recipe a try (pg. 32). We're giving you the classic Italian version and our own Bite Club version (which one could argue is just a stuffed sandwich).

TRADITIONAL

- **Tapenade Spread (from pg. 24)**
- **1 round bread loaf (about 7 inches in diameter and 3 inches high)**
- **4 oz. thinly sliced Genoa salami**
- **4 oz. thinly sliced cooked ham**
- **4 oz. sliced mortadella**
- **4 oz. sliced mozzarella cheese**
- **4 z. sliced provolone cheese**

BITE CLUB STYLE

- **BC Style Tapenade Spread (from pg. 24)**
- **1 round bread loaf (about 7 inches in diameter and 3 inches high)**
- **4 oz. black forest ham**
- **4 oz. smoked turkey**
- **4 oz. thinly sliced chicken**
- **4 oz. sliced mozzarella cheese**
- **4 oz. sliced smoked provolone cheese**
- **thinly sliced red onion**
- **dill pickle slices**

Slice the bread horizontally. If it's a thicker loaf, gut some of the bread from the inside, leaving a rim around the edge. This is to serve as a catch so when you bite into it, all the ingredients don't go sliding out the back on you.

Start by coating both halves in the tapenade, then layer in this order:

TRADITIONAL - provolone, mortadella, ham, salami, mozzarella

BC STYLE - provolone, chicken, pickles, turkey, onion, ham, mozzarella

Place top half of bread on. You now have a few options on how to eat this beast!

Option 1 - Wrap tightly in plastic wrap or foil and let sit for 6-8 hours. This is the traditional way and allows the oils and acids from the tapenade to seep through the soft interior of the bread and really meld the flavors.

OPTION 2 - Preheat oven to 300°F. Wrap sandwich tightly in foil and heat for 15-20 minutes to allow the cheese to slightly melt and lock everything together.

OPTION 3 - Just start noshing. While the sandwich is good, option 1 or 2 will give you a much brighter, bolder flavor profile.

THE KORRITO

The Ultimate Fusion

Take Americas love of the burrito and stuff it full with Asian flavors and you have a hand-held delicacy that will have you drooling for more. The original inception was more sushi style wrapped in a big sheet of nori. More recent styles fuse bulgogi beef and sticky rice with kimchi in a flour tortilla shell.

INGREDIENTS

BEEF MARINADE

- ⅓ Cup soy sauce
- 2 Tablespoons sugar
- 1 Tablespoon toasted sesame oil
- ½ of a pear, peeled, cored, and coarsely grated
- 5 medium cloves garlic, minced or grated
- 1 Tablespoon minced ginger
- 1 ½ lbs. ribeye, top round, or sirloin, very thinly sliced against the grain, cut into thin strips
- 3 green onions, white and light green parts only, diced
- ¼ of a yellow onion, finely diced
- 2 Tablespoons vegetable or canola oil

FILLINGS

- 4 large flour tortillas, warmed
- 4 Cups cooked short-grain rice
- 1 Cup sour cream
- 1 Tablespoon gochujang chili paste
- chopped kimchi (homemade or store bought)
- daikon, sliced into thin strips
- 2 Cups finely shredded red cabbage
- 2 Cups cilantro leaves, chopped

DIRECTIONS

MARINATE THE BEEF: In a large bowl, whisk together soy sauce, sugar, sesame oil, pear, garlic, and ginger and stir till sugar dissolves. Add beef, green onions, and yellow onion to the bowl and toss to coat. Cover and refrigerate for at least 1 hour or overnight.

In a large skillet, heat 1 Tablespoon oil over medium-high heat, coating bottom of pan.

Dump the bowl of marinade and beef into a strainer, then add beef and onions to skillet. Don't overcrowd the pan, if you need to do this in multiple batches, that's fine. You want the beef as a single layer on the pan bottom. Cook for 1 minute, then flip and cook for another 2 minutes.

In a bowl, stir together sour cream and gochujang. Spread rice onto warm tortillas, then top with a layer of beef and onions, followed by kimchi, a few daikon strips, red cabbage, cilantro, and gochujang sour cream mix. Roll tightly, folding sides of tortilla in as you go.

Feel free to wrap this up in a nori sheet, but if you do, I would suggest using sushi rice or another "sticky" short grain rice.

Chicken Pesto Panini

Grilled Chicken & Pesto is the Besto!

Savory pesto just brings out the best in chicken. Works with grilled or baked chicken. If you don't have a grill/panini press, you can heat up 2 pans and press the sandwich between them. Cast iron pans will, of course, be the best for this. Or grab a brick from outside, wash and sanitize it, then wrap it in foil for a great sandwich/chicken/bacon/burger press!

INGREDIENTS

- 2 chicken breasts, grilled/roasted/baked
- 2 ciabatta rolls or 4 slices thick Italian bread (we recommend Turano, available at most markets)
- ¼ Cup pesto (homemade or bought)
- 1 tomato, thinly sliced
- 4 oz. fresh mozzarella, thinly sliced
- olive oil
- salt and pepper

MAKE YOUR OWN PESTO!

- ½ Cup toasted pine nuts, almonds, walnuts, pistachios, pecans, hemp seeds, or pipetas
- 2 Tablespoons lemon juice
- ¼ teaspoon sea salt and pepper
- 2 large garlic cloves
- 2 Cups fresh basil leaves, mint, spinach, parsley, or cilantro
- ¼ Cup extra-virgin olive oil
- ¼ Cup grated parmesan cheese

In a food processor, add the nuts, lemon juice, garlic, salt, pepper, and pulse in bursts until well chopped.

Throw in the chosen leafy greens and pulse it again until combined.

Drizzle in the olive oil while the processor is running and blend until combined. Throw in the parmesan cheese and pulse to briefly combine. If you would like a "smoother" pesto, drizzle in more olive oil.

If you find your pesto is "too sharp", drizzle a bit of honey into the food processor and pulse once or twice to combine.

DIRECTIONS

Grill/roast/bake your chicken breasts sprinkled with a bit of oregano, basil, or an Italian spice blend. Slice into strips after cooking.

Slice ciabatta rolls in half, then spread about ¼ of the pesto on bottom half of each roll. Top with tomato, sliced chicken, and mozzarella. Spread remaining pesto on the top half of each roll and close.

COOKING IN A PAN: Heat a pan with 2 Tablespoons oil and add paninis. Cook until bottom is golden and cheese starts to melt, about 5 minutes. Flip, then place a heavy skillet or your new cooking brick on top of sandwich and press down to flatten panini. Cook another 5 minutes.

PANINI PRESS: Brush outer sides of paninis with olive oil. Place in press and close, applying pressure to the top plate to flatten panini. Cook until bread is golden and cheese is melting.

HAWAiiAN INSPiReD PuLled ChiCKEN SANDWiCHES

Aloha Bitches!

Taking our pulled chicken in a slightly different direction. Traditionally shredded, we've also cubed this chicken after cooking and served it over our Hawaiian Fried Rice (pg. 90) in a halved, hollowed out pineapple.

INGREDiENTS

Chicken

- 1 ½ lbs. skinless, boneless chicken breasts or thighs
- 1 Tablespoon chili powder
- 1 teaspoon sweet paprika
- 1 Tablespoon brown sugar
- Kosher salt and freshly ground black pepper
- 2 Tablespoons extra-virgin olive oil
- 1 medium red onion, chopped
- 3 cloves garlic, minced
- ½ Cup pineapple preserves
- 3 Tablespoons yellow mustard
- 1 Cup pineapple juice
- 1 Tablespoon apple cider vinegar
- 6 hamburger buns, lightly toasted

Hula Slaw

- (1) 14-oz. bag shredded coleslaw mix
- 1 red bell pepper, very thinly sliced
- Kosher salt and freshly ground black pepper
- ½ Cup unsweetened coconut flakes, toasted
- 2 green onions thinly sliced
- 4 Tablespoons fresh cilantro, chopped (or 2 Tablespoons dried)
- ⅓ Cup mayonnaise
- 3 Tablespoons apple cider vinegar

DiRECTiONS

Season the chicken with salt and pepper and let sit for 5 minutes while you mix the rub. Mix the chili powder, paprika, and brown sugar in a bowl and rub all over the chicken. Set your pressure cooker to sauté. Add the oil, then the chicken, and cook, turning until browned, about 3 minutes. Transfer to a plate. Add the red onion to the pot and cook, about 5 minutes. Make sure to scrape up any browned bits from the bottom of the pot with a wooden spoon. That is tasty gold! Add garlic during the last minute of cooking. Cancel the sauté setting.

Pop that chicken back in the pot. Whisk the preserves, 2 Tablespoons mustard, and the pineapple juice in a small bowl; pour over the chicken and give it a stir. Put on the lid, seal the steam valve, and set the cooker to high pressure for 8 minutes. When finished, carefully vent to release the pressure. Transfer the chicken to a plate and shred the meat into large chunks with 2 forks or meat claws.

Set the cooker back to sauté. Bring the sauce to a simmer and cook for about 8 minutes, or until the sauce is reduced to about half. Return the shredded chicken to the pot and stir to coat. Continue to cook, stirring occasionally, until almost all the sauce is absorbed, about 10 more minutes. Stir in the remaining Tablespoon of mustard and the vinegar.

To craft the slaw: Toss the coleslaw mix and bell pepper with ½ teaspoon salt and a few grinds of black pepper. Let stand 5 minutes. Add the coconut, green onions, cilantro, mayonnaise, and vinegar and toss to coat.

Divide the chicken among the buns and top with some of the slaw.

FRIED CHICKEN SAMMICH

Everyone else has a fried chicken sandwich...

We keep it simple with the flavors and let the marinated chicken speak for itself. Plan ahead for this one, as there is some marinating time to take into account.

INGREDIENTS

- ½ Cup pickle juice
- 2 teaspoons Kosher salt, divided
- 1 teaspoon paprika
- 1 teaspoon chili powder
- 1 teaspoon black pepper
- ½ teaspoon garlic powder
- ½ teaspoon onion powder
- 1 ½ lbs. boneless, skinless chicken thighs or breasts
- 1 Cup buttermilk (or 1 Cup milk + 1 Tablespoon of vinegar or lemon juice, stirred and left standing for 10 minutes)
- ¼ Cup cheap vodka
- 1 large egg
- 2 Cups all-purpose flour
- ¼ Cup cornstarch
- 1 Tablespoon salt
- 1 Tablespoon pepper
- Peanut/vegetable/canola oil, for frying
- 6 hamburger buns
- lettuce, tomatoes, pickles, mayo

DIRECTIONS

Mix pickle juice, salt, paprika, pepper, chili powder, garlic powder, and onion powder in a gallon-size zip top plastic bag. Drop in the chicken, seal it, and give it a good mushing around to make sure all the chicken is coated. Place in refrigerator for at least 2 hours or overnight.

Whisk together buttermilk, vodka, and egg in a large bowl. Remove chicken from brine and pat dry with paper towels. Add chicken to buttermilk mixture.

Whisk together flour, cornstarch, remaining 1 Tablespoon salt, and remaining 1 Tablespoon black pepper in shallow dish. Set aside.

Pour oil in a tall pot at least an inch deep, or preheat your deep fryer. Heat oil to at least 375°F.

Working in batches, remove 3 or 4 pieces of chicken from buttermilk and place in flour mixture. Cover chicken with flour mixture, pressing to adhere. Lift from flour mixture and gently shake off excess. Carefully place chicken in hot oil, taking care not to overcrowd pot or fryer basket. Try to keep oil temperature above 350°F. Turn chicken every 1 to 2 minutes using tongs, until a thermometer inserted into the thickest portion of meat registers 165°F and breading is golden brown and very crispy, 6 to 8 minutes per batch. Remove chicken from oil and place on a wire rack set inside a rimmed baking sheet. Place in preheated 200°F oven to keep warm while repeating frying process with remaining chicken.

Brush butter on each side of bun and toast in a dry pan over medium heat till golden brown. Pile on the toppings of your choice.

SRIRACHA MAYO IS AMAZING ON A FRIED CHICKEN SANDWICH. JUST MIX ¼ CUP OF YOUR FAVORITE MAYO WITH 1 TABLESPOON OF SRIRACHA. SPREAD ON BUN TOPS AND BOTTOMS.

CHEESESTEAK SAMMICH

Not making these is a cheesy mis-steak!!!

Tons of debate over the proper way to craft these iconic Philly sandwiches. Cheesewhiz, provolone, or American... onions or peppers or even mushrooms. Seasonings or just S&P... the beauty of these is as long as you get a decent cut of meat, make it your own!

DIRECTIONS

Heat a griddle or a large sauté pan over medium-high heat. When hot, drizzle in olive oil.

Add the onions and bell pepper and cook, stirring until caramelized, about 8 minutes. Add the garlic, salt, and pepper; cook for about 30 seconds. Pile this mixture on one side of the griddle or pan.

Add the meat to the pan or griddle. Cook by continuously flipping the meat over until the meat is no longer pink, about 2-3 minutes depending on thickness.

Then mix the meat with veggies in the pan/griddle. Divide into 2 piles and top with cheese.

While cheese is melting, cut the bread in half, crosswise, and slice lengthwise to open. Hollow out some of the soft white bread part from inside and place the bread face down on top of the meat and cheese.

When the cheese is melted, slide a spatula under the pile, and holding onto the top of the bread, flip the sandwiches over.

INGREDIENTS

- **2 large French or Italian sub rolls, toasted**
- **½ lb. rib-eye, top round, bottom round, or sirloin, sliced super thin (ask the butcher counter at your local grocery store to slice it wafer thin)**
- **1 yellow onion, sliced thin**
- **1 green bell pepper, sliced thin**
- **2 teaspoons minced garlic**
- **½ lb. provolone cheese, sliced thin**
- **olive oil**
- **salt and pepper**

> YOU CAN MAKE THIS A CHICKEN CHEESESTEAK SANDWICH! JUST REPLACE THE BEEF WITH THINLY SLICED STRIPS OF CHICKEN. EVERYTHING ELSE IS THE SAME!

> FAJITA CHEESESTEAK? SWAP OUT THE GREEN PEPPER FOR A MIX OF THINLY SLICED RED AND ORANGE PEPPERS. ADD IN 2 TABLESPOONS OF LIME JUICE AND 2 TABLESPOONS OF FAJITA SEASONING WHEN YOU ADD THE MEAT TO THE PAN! SWAP THE PROVOLONE FOR SLICED PEPPER-JACK.

> FEEL FREE TO ADD IN 8 OZ. OF SLICED MUSHROOMS INTO THE PAN WITH THE PEPPERS AND ONIONS. SWAP OUT THE CHEESES (CHEF TONY DIGS MOZZARELLA ON HIS). GIVE THE MEAT A SPLASH OF WORCESTERSHIRE IN THE PAN. MAKE IT YOUR OWN!!!

PALATE FATIGUE:
Too Much of a Good Thing??

Palate Fatigue or "taste bud exhaustion" or the more scientific sounding "sensory enervation" occurs when tasting a multitude of comparable products consecutively.

Mostly dominant in the professional world of competitive coffee and wine taste testers, this concept can be applied to almost anything you nosh, sip, devour, or jam into your cheeks like a squirrel in October.

Basically, your taste buds and nose are just overworked. Scientists actually believe it's our brain that becomes fatigued, not our taste buds. Think of your brain like a computer. You are editing a picture, rendering some 3D animation, sending unsolicited pictures through DM, and uploading that cute picture of your cat to social media while streaming the latest album by your favorite Finnish Death Metal band... at some point, something is going to get locked up. Same thing happens to food and your brain. A fat burger with a rich aioli, loaded with tomatoes, thick cut bacon, and mushrooms may be the greatest thing you ever noshed... for the first 3 bites. Then it'll start tasting like... well... kinda like nothing. And that burger is fine, it's your brain that is diminishing the flavor. Stupid brain!

So how do we combat that? The easiest way is with a palate cleanser.

A palate cleanser is a neutral flavored food or drink that helps remove food residue from the mouth and taste bud receptors, and "reboots" your palate so the mouth, nose, and brain can more accurately assess the flavors.

Ever wonder why they drop a small plate of pickled ginger off with your sushi? It's meant to be a palate cleanser between rolls. Sorbet in between courses at an upper-class restaurant? It's not dessert, it's a palate cleanser.

Sorbet is often the go-to palate cleanser because it's very light, "clean tasting", and made with lighter, acidic flavors. Sorbet is often made without, or very little, sweeteners, so it doesn't add to the onslaught of the taste buds. Lemon and lime are often the popular choices (acidic) and refreshes the mouth, especially after fattier foods.

Other popular palate cleansers are bread, crackers, apples, bananas, pickles, and tea.

But it's silly if you are tearing into a fat ass burger and think the burger joint will have a small cup of sorbet waiting for you... so just rely on one of the best palate cleansers available everywhere.

Water.

After a few bites, sip some water, and wait a minute or two before tearing into it again. The flavors will be refreshed and your taste buds rebooted.

And there are other types of palate fatigue! Ever walk into a department store and start sniffing colognes and perfumes? Or candles? After smelling a couple, they all start smelling the same! Since smell and taste are intertwined, this type of fatigue affects the nasal palate.

There is also flavor fatigue which occurs when you enjoy the same flavor "profile" constantly. Your poor taste buds have just been pushed to the limits of tolerance for the same food/flavors.

CULINARY SCIENCE BREAK!

You are going to hear the word "*Maillard*" (pronounced as mə-'lärd) tossed about in this book, so it's important to know exactly what in the Cinnamon Toast Fuck it means.

Ever eaten a steak seared to perfection? Drank coffee? Used condensed milk? Munched on some fries? Enjoy a crusty loaf of bread? A soft brioche? Dig grilled onions on your burger or dog? Enjoy a malt beer or malt whiskey with dinner? Relaxed by a campfire making S'Mores?

All of these have 1 thing in common: The Maillard Reaction.

Discovered by French chemist Louis Camille Maillard in the early 1900s, the Maillard Reaction is the non-enzymatic reaction that occurs in the presence of heat between amino acids and reducing sugars that results in flavor, texture, and aromas. Water plays a huge role in the reaction (more water = less reaction, that's why you pat your steaks dry before searing). To put it simply: Protein + Sugar + Heat = Maillard Reaction. It begins at about 280°F but doesn't start rocking until about 320°F, although many culinary scientists disagree at what temperature in that range it *actually* starts taking place.

The Maillard Reaction can be broken down into 3 stages: early, advanced, and final. We always aim for early and advanced. You'll know when you hit the final stage, as whatever you are cooking will look like it was cooked in Satan's asshole. Usually inedible. Smoke alarms going off. Probably ruined a pan in the process.

During the process, hundreds of different flavor compounds are created. Then those compounds break down and form even more new flavor compounds, and so on. On a side note, it's those compounds that scientists have used over the years to create artificial flavors. Umami is built on this, that savory, mouthwatering flavor that makes you drool (more on umami later in the book).

The Maillard Reaction can also be accomplished at lower temps with a lot more water. Take chicken stock. Low heat and gallons of water left to simmer for hours will produce a beautiful and delicious light brown stock. That's the Maillard Reaction in the early stage.

The Maillard Reaction can also be hacked. By raising the pH (adding baking soda), you'll create richer flavor and aroma compounds. Lowering pH (adding acid) or raising the temp will result in a crispier crust. Pan frying or deep frying is the best of both of these worlds.

Oh, want to know why you crave chicken and waffles? Because they represent BOTH sides of the Maillard Reaction. Waffles are sugar heavy and packed with aroma, but low on flavor, whereas fried chicken is the opposite. Then toss in some maple syrup or honey and BOOM... now wipe your chin.

BURGERS

"Food rules. Little rivals the pleasure of tearing into a glistening burger."

- Mary H. K. Choi

"We all need to make time for a burger once in a while."

- Erica Durance

"Eat clean to stay fit; have a burger to stay sane."

- Gigi Hadid

"The best stories are like the best burgers: Big, juicy and messy."

- A.D. Posey

WELCOME TO THE GRIND...

I promise... once you grind your own beef, you'll never go back to prepackaged ground proteins again.

Look, I get it. Grinding your own meat is a daunting, intimidating, time intensive task for most. You need a meat grinder, gotta know what meats to use, and know how to eyeball the fat content.... I understand how temping that 1 lb. package of pre-ground beef is. I won't judge... busy households need something quick. Feel free to use pre-ground beef in any of my recipes if it fits better for your household.

But if you want to really elevate your burgers, tacos, meatloaf, sloppy joes, etc... all it will take is a little investment. And you can grind and freeze batches so you'll always have it on hand! There's a lot to grind out *(I'm so funny),* so let's get to it!

So why grind?

There are two main reasons: **customization and cost.** Grinding your own meat allows you to customize the flavor by using different cuts of meat (we will get into that in a bit). This gives you the advantage of knowing exactly what is in your meat. The prepackaged stuff is usually a mix of different cuts... and stores don't need to disclose what cuts. They also don't disclose to you that prepackaged meats are often pumped with carbon monoxide to keep that appealing red coloring and extend shelf life!

The second is cost. Meat prices these days are all over the place, and right now that package of 93/7 is probably averaging about $6.50 a pound. A chuck roast (most popular for grinding) is about $4.99 a pound. Since those roasts usually come out at 3-5 lbs. at the grocery store, at minimum you've just doubled the amount of ground beef for the same price without any filler meats or gasses pumped in.

Let's talk shop.

A meat grinder doesn't have to be a wallet breaking investment. If you already have a stand mixer, basic meat grinder attachments go for about $30 bucks online. Metal encased ones go for a bit more, around $50-70. If you don't have a stand mixer, decent self-contained electric ones start around $100. Or, you can use your food processor (but the texture won't be nearly as good).

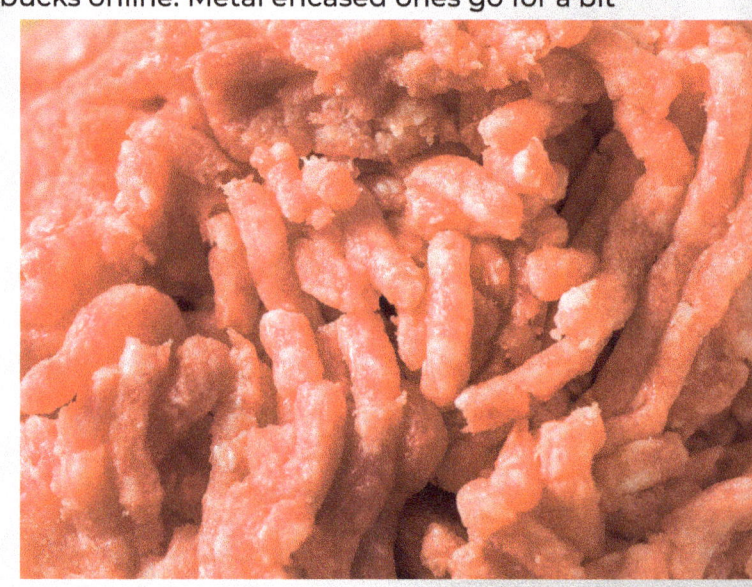

When I first started grinding my own meat, I had a plastic meat grinding attachment for the stand mixer. I'd run 10 lbs. of meat through it with no problems once every 3 weeks.

Once you grind about 15 lbs. of meat, that grinder just paid for itself.

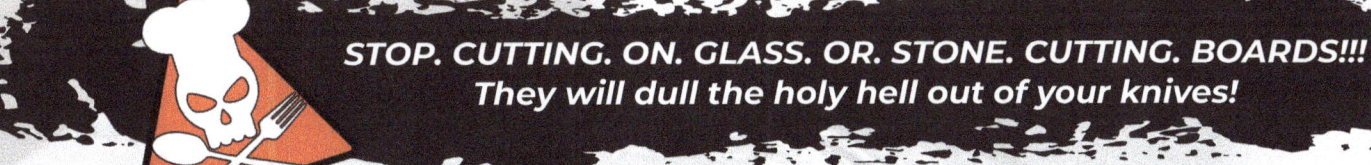
Ratios and Percentages

Awesome, fresh ground burger meats have 3 things in common - *FLAVOR*, *TEXTURE*, and *FAT*. And I know... the evil "F" word; but just remember that over half the fat in beef is monounsaturated... you know, the heart healthy kind also found in olive oil. So, here's the target fat content you should be aiming for in your fresh ground beef for burgers: 25-30%. This will result in the juiciest, most mouth watering burgers you've ever jammed in your maw. If you like your burgers medium well (sigh), aim for 40%. And if you like your burgers still moo'ing, a 20% fat ratio will be just fine.

And before you freak out over a rare burger, remember... YOU ground the meat. YOU know exactly what went into it. YOU did all the handling. It's the absolute safest way to enjoy a rare burger.

THE MEATY DETAILS

Here are some of the common cuts used for grinding:

Chuck - This is a solid starting point. The lean-to-fat ratio is almost perfect, at 23-25%. You could technically just use this cut for your burgers, but to ramp it up to that perfect ratio, add a bit of round or sirloin to bring it to mouthwatering perfection. Here in Bite Club, our magic number is a 4:1 ratio of chuck to round.

Boneless Short Ribs - perfect fat content for grinding (30%) and a rich flavor, adding this into the mix will deliver a very savory, moist burger.

Brisket - at 25% fat content, a perfect addition to add to round or sirloin.

Tri-tip, Sirloin, and Round - All relatively lean cuts, with tri-tip at 12%, sirloin at 18%, and round at about 12-14%. You technically *can* grind these alone for leaner beef, but don't use solely for burgers. Use these where other fats will be introduced, like for taco meat.

Skirt and Hanger steak - at 15-17%, these leaner yet tougher cuts will bring a "tangier" beef flavor that will be recognized when bit into. A 1:1 skirt/chuck combo is magical.

Basic Grinding Guidelines.

-Chill the grinder- Pop the tray, chute, spiral, and grinding disks in the freezer for at least an hour before you start grinding. All accessories need to be very cold. Why? You gotta keep the meat cold during grinding.

-Chill the Meat- Slice the raw meat into 1" cubes, spread on a sheet pan, and toss in the freezer for 20-30 minutes. You want that meat firm (hehe) not frozen.

-Cold Bowls- You are gonna need a cold bowl to catch the ground meat. If you have the room in the freezer, just toss the bowl in there with the grinder parts. If not, dump ice into a large bowl, then place a smaller bowl inside that one on top of the ice.

-Grind, then Grind Again- Most grinders come with 2-3 grinding plates that vary with different size holes. Run the cubed steak through with the plate that has the largest holes first. Then swap it out for a plate with smaller holes and run the ground beef through for a second time (this step is incredibly important if you are making our Smashed Burgers).

FOOD PROCESSOR METHOD - Cube and chill the beef as described before. Then in batches, pulse the meat until finely chopped. Dump into chilled bowls and do the next batch.

The key from here on out is to handle the meat with your hands as little as possible, because the more you handle your meat *...crickets...*, the denser it will be after cooking. Plus, if you are anything like me, your hands run hot in the kitchen. Hot hands + raw meat are not a good combo.

For standard burgers: loosely grab 4-6oz., gently form it into a patty, and make an indentation in the top with your thumb. This will keep the meat from swelling and hold that "patty" shape during cooking. Refrigerate for around 30 minutes. *DO NOT SALT* at this point. Salt draws moisture out. We can season later. Also, do not add liquids like smoke or Worcestershire to the mix. Liquids will prevent the meat from holding together.

For Smash Burgers: grab 3-4 oz. of meat, form it into a rough ball. Refrigerate.

For "loose meat" dishes (tacos, pasta sauce, etc.): season and use.

For Freezing: A vacuum sealer would be the best to use. If you don't have access to one, place meat into a zip top bag and lower into water to the top of the bag. Don't let water run in the bag. The pressure of the water will squeeze most of all the air out.

Air + Freezer = Freezer Burn

You are ready... Let's Grind!

OK! You got the grinder and all its parts chilling in the freezer. The meat is cubed and in the freezer to firm up. Do everything you need to do to clear up the next 25 minutes of your life. Once you start, there's a bit of urgency to run through it as quickly as possible. The danger temperature zone for meat is between 40-140°F. This is where bacteria grow the fastest. Your hands will generate heat, the grinder will generate heat, and unless you are grinding in a walk-in freezer, your house is probably at a comfortable temperature well inside that danger zone.

So check your phone, reply to emails, feed the pets, put on music, and read to the end of this page. Because for the next 25 minutes your life is on that grinder!

If you choose to wear gloves while doing this, make sure they are powder free. You don't have to wear gloves if you don't mind the feel of raw meat, just wash your hands for 30 seconds with a great antibacterial soap right before you start grabbing the meat (ohh the puns).

Ready?

Pull the grinder parts from the freezer and attach them to the mixer, or in the case of a free-standing grinder, attach the shoot to the base. Position your cold catch bowl underneath the dispenser. Grab the meat from the freezer, click on the grinder, and start feeding it through the tube, using the pusher to make sure it goes down.

All done? A little trick I learned from a great butcher is to grab 1 or 2 slices of bread and push them down the grinder tube. The bread will help push the last bits of meat through the plate without altering the meat in any way.

Unscrew the holding cap on the grinder and take out the grinding plate. Replace it with the next size or two down. Reattach the holding cap, and start feeding that ground meat through the grinder again. What you will be left with are fine strands of the best damn ground beef you've ever had. Lastly, run a few more slices of bread through to push out the last of the meat.

You'll probably ground more then you will need, so wrap up the extras in freezer paper in 1 lb. blocks, and freeze them in freezer zip-top bags or vacuum bags. Pack them as flat as possible, they will defrost faster that way. The frozen meat will stay delicious for at least 6-12 months.

BC'S SMASHED BURGERS

The heart of the Bite Club Kitchen

We were always told never to press down on a burger. We were also told eating carrots would give us super night vision. The world is full of bullshit. Say hello to your new favorite burger.

INGREDIENTS

- **fresh ground beef (3-4oz. of meat per burger)**
- **salt**
- **pepper**

I'll state this once again, fresh ground beef will always be superior. Better taste, better texture. If you don't want to grind your own, head to your local grocery store and get some fresh ground beef from the meat counter. That is usually ground fresh in the morning and isn't subjected to stacking and customers manhandling.

You can totally make these burgers with pre-packaged ground beef, but the texture of your burgers will be completely different. Not a bad thing per say... just different. Also with pre-packed beef or turkey, you may have to add a few more spices to cover or enhance the "duller" flavors. Some onion powder and a splash of Worcestershire sauce is a classic go to, cause they add a pop of umami. And remember, handle the meat (snicker) as little as possible. It's already been compressed together in the packaging for a while.

DIRECTIONS

Form the beef into 3-4oz. LOOSE balls.

Get a flattop or skillet ripping with heat. When hot, paint the surface with a bit of butter.

Place the ball of meat on the flattop or skillet, and with either the back of a solid spatula, a burger weight, a bacon press, or a clean brick wrapped in foil, smash that burger for about 15-30 seconds. Don't press so hard that the meat squirts completely out from under your weight. You are making burgers... not meat paper.

After 15-30 seconds, peek underneath the burger. It should be "caramelized" if the heat was high enough. If not, just let it cook but DON'T smash again. Once the bottom is caramelized to your liking, flip it over and cook till caramelized.

Serve dressed as desired.

Want to go beyond good ol' ketchup and mustard? Give our Burger Sauce on pg. 24 a try and experience a whole new depth of flavor!

TURKEY BURGER

Don't listen to the haters...

The Turkey Burger gets a bad rap, and for good reason. No one puts the work into making it decent! You can't treat it like regular ground beef. But I'm here to tell you that a turkey burger can be a pretty kick ass burger! Bonus... it's smashable!

INGREDIENTS

- 1 lb. lean ground turkey
- ½ medium onion
- 1 Tablespoon plain dried breadcrumbs
- 1 teaspoon salt
- ½ teaspoon freshly ground black pepper
- ½ teaspoon garlic powder
- ½ teaspoon onion powder
- ¼ teaspoon chili powder
- 1 Tablespoon Worcestershire sauce
- 2 Tablespoons ketchup

DIRECTIONS

Grate the onion over the fine holes of a grater. Discard the juice it leaves behind (there will be a LOT, you can also save it and throw it into your enemy's eyes), and squeeze as much liquid out of the onion shavings as possible. Toss the onion in a bowl with all the other ingredients and mix gently with your hands until fully incorporated into the turkey. The meat should be somewhat moist and slightly sticky to the touch. If it's really wet, add another Tablespoon or 2 of bread crumbs. Certain brands of ground turkey are "wetter" then others, so some adjustment is needed.

Form the patties into 4 oz. balls, then gently smash into a patty shape.

Oil the grill grates, cast iron pan, flattop, or grill press and cook for about 5 minutes per side, or until the internal temperature reads 160°F and let it rest for a few minutes. It will continue to cook to 165°F (safe temp.) and be so juicy! If cooking on a flattop or skillet, you can smash these babies further.

NOTES ON YOUR STINKY FINGERS...

If you use your hands to squeeze out the onion juice, they are going to stink. After you ask a few people to smell your finger, you are gonna want to get the smell off your digits. If you have a stainless-steel sink, just rub your hands on the metal for about 10 seconds, then wash with soap and water. The stank should be mostly gone (this also works for garlic... but no one ever complains about that). If you plan on working with onions and garlic a lot, you may want to invest in a "Stainless Steel Soap Bar" available online for around $10.

Black Bean Burgers

The perfect burger for Meatless Mondays

Calm down haters. Just because you had a crappy one once at a chain restaurant doesn't mean these can't be pretty damn awesome. The secret is roasting the beans before smooshing them up to bring out the flavor and get rid of excess moisture. Oh look, you can smash these as well!

INGREDIENTS

- 28 oz. (or 2 cans) black beans, drained, rinsed, and patted dry
- 1 Tablespoon extra-virgin olive oil
- ½ large yellow onion, finely chopped
- ½ bell pepper, finely chopped
- 4 garlic cloves, minced
- 2 teaspoons ground cumin
- 1 ½ teaspoons chili powder
- 1 teaspoon garlic powder
- ½ teaspoon smoked paprika
- ½ Cup bread crumbs
- 2 large eggs
- 1 Tablespoon Worcestershire sauce
- 1 teaspoon liquid smoke
- 2 Tablespoons ketchup or BBQ Sauce
- salt and pepper

Feel free to play with the spices here! Instead of ketchup or BBQ sauce, replace with sriracha. Swap the cumin with fajita seasoning! Use flavored breadcrumbs. For umami, swap the Worcestershire for A.1. Sauce or oyster sauce for a new spin on flavor. Leave out the liquid smoke and try sprinkling on smoked salts.

DIRECTIONS

Preheat oven to 325°F and dump the beans onto an aluminum foil lined baking sheet and bake for 15 minutes. You'll see some splitting open or cracking. This is good.

While the beans are roasting, heat the oil in a pan and sauté the peppers and onions over medium heat until soft, about 5-6 minutes. During the last minute, add the garlic. Dump the pan in a food processor with the remaining ingredients and pulse everything together. Remove top and add the black beans, pulsing in bursts. You want the mixture to pull together while still leaving some larger chunks of the beans.

Form into 4-6 oz. patties, roughly the size of your buns. These will not shrink on the grill like animal proteins, so don't make them bigger then the buns to compensate.

Place patties on flattop, in grill press, or in a pan and cook until outside is starting to get crispy. You can also bake these at 375°F for 10 minutes per side.

NOTE: *Black Bean Burgers are more delicate then regular burgers, so if you plan on popping these on a grill, place them on greased heavy-duty aluminum foil and grill over medium high heat for 8 minutes per side. Once cooked, you can remove them from the foil and place them delicately on the hot grates to get the grill marks charred in.*

Luau Burger with Spam & Sweet & Spicy Slaw

A vacation for the taste buds!

Sweet pineapple, savory lean beef, and SPAM come together for a burger that captures the Hawaiian Spirit while delivering contrasting flavors and textures in a unique and delicious way! Serve these up on Hawaiian burger buns with a Mai Tai at your next luau!

INGREDIENTS

'Ino a maika 'i ka Slaw *(Naughty and Nice Slaw)*

- 3 thick fresh or canned pineapple rings
- granulated sugar
- 1-2 fresh jalapeños
- 1 Cup shredded cabbage
- 4 chopped green onions
- 2 Tablespoons honey
- 2 Tablespoons sesame oil
- ½ teaspoon Kosher salt
- 4 Tablespoons rice vinegar
- ½ Tablespoon toasted sesame seeds

BURGERS

- 1 Tablespoon soy sauce
- 2 Tablespoons honey
- 1 can of SPAM
- 1 lb. ground sirloin (90/10)
- 1 teaspoon sweet paprika
- 1 teaspoon onion powder
- 1 teaspoon Kosher salt
- ½ teaspoon black pepper
- 2 Tablespoons melted butter
- 4 Hawaiian style hamburger buns

DIRECTIONS

Preheat grill to high and oil the grates. Coat each side of pineapple rings with sugar, place on grill, and cook until deeply caramelized, 3 minutes per side. Grill jalapeño until charred, 2 minutes a side, until blackish blistering on all sides. Brush melted butter on all inside halves of buns and toast on grill.

Remove pineapple and jalapeño from grill and finely chop. Place in bowl with cabbage, vinegar, green onions, sesame oil, honey, and salt. Give it a good toss to combine. This can be made an hour ahead of time. Store in fridge till ready to use.

Burger time! Stir together honey and soy sauce in a shallow dish. Slice SPAM into 8 slices (lengthwise) and brush both sides of SPAM with honey/soy sauce mixture. Form beef into 4 oz. patties, sprinkle with salt, pepper, and paprika. Place SPAM and burgers on oiled grates and cook till desired doneness. Brush SPAM with sauce mix once more while cooking. Build in this order: bun, burger, SPAM, slaw, bun top.

Buffalo Chicken Burger

AKA: The inside out Wing Burger

We took the classic Buffalo Wing and turned it inside out to create this burger perfect for tailgating, cookouts, or just because your local wing shack is closed! If the idea of bleu cheese creeps you out, you can use feta to achieve that sharp taste.

INGREDIENTS

- 1 lb ground chicken
- 2 Tablespoons green onion, finely chopped
- 3 garlic cloves, minced
- pinch of salt and a few grinds of black pepper
- 2 teaspoons fresh minced parsley (or 1 teaspoon dried parsley)
- bread crumbs (optional if needed)
- Buffalo Sauce (recipe on page)
- crumbled bleu cheese or feta
- ranch dressing
- hamburger buns

IF PAN COOKING

- 1 Tablespoon flour
- 1 Tablespoon cornstarch

BITE CLUB'S BUFFALO SAUCE!

- 1 stick unsalted butter
- 1 Cup Franks Red Hot or Louisiana Hot Sauce
- 1 ½ Tablespoons vinegar
- Splash of Worcestershire
- ¼ teaspoon garlic powder
- ¼ teaspoon red pepper (depending on how hot you want it or omit for a mild sauce)
- pinch of salt

Throw all ingredients in a pot over medium heat and bring to a simmer. Gently continue to stir with a whisk. When you see simmering bubbles start appearing, kill the heat. If too thin, continue to simmer a bit to thicken.

DIRECTIONS

Mix ground chicken, onion, garlic, parsley, salt, and pepper. If you find your mixture to be a bit on the wetter side (as different chicken brands vary in moisture), mix in bread crumbs to help balance it out. Form into patties and store in fridge for at least 2 hours to firm them up.

Rock the grill to medium and oil the grates. Grill 4 to 6 minutes per side or until cooked through. Flip the burgers only once during grilling. Top cooked side with buffalo sauce, followed by cheese, and allow cheese to melt. Butter and toast the bun on the grill. Top with ranch and serve with carrot and celery sticks.

To pan fry: Heat skillet to medium high. Add oil to the pan. While oil is heating up, dust the burgers with a mixture of the flour and cornstarch, both sides. When oil is hot, add burgers. Cook 4 to 5 minutes per side, flip once. Add buffalo sauce then cheese to the burger. Place lid on skillet to melt cheese. Top with the ranch and serve with carrot and celery sticks.

Mongolian Turkey Burger with Tangy Apple Slaw

Flavors of the East styled by the West

Confucius once said, "Everyone eats and drinks, yet only few appreciate the taste of food." Well, this burger will make you take notice of the sweet, the sour, the tangy, the savory, and the perfection that is this killer turkey burger.

INGREDIENTS

- 3 green onions, minced
- 2 garlic cloves, minced
- 1 Tablespoon minced fresh ginger (or ½ Tablespoon ginger powder)
- 2 Tablespoons hoisin sauce
- ½ teaspoon salt
- ½ teaspoon pepper
- 1 ¼ lbs. ground turkey
- ½ Tablespoon sesame oil

APPLE SLAW:

- 2 medium Fuji apples, julienned (or any sweet apple will do, such as Kiku, Gala, Honeycrisp, Jazz, Braeburn, etc.)
- 2 green onions, finely chopped
- ½ Tablespoon fresh ginger
- 2 Tablespoons apple cider vinegar
- 1 Tablespoon seasoned rice vinegar
- 1 teaspoon Dijon mustard
- ¼ teaspoon salt
- ¼ teaspoon pepper

DIRECTIONS

Stir together the first 6 ingredients. Add turkey. With your hands, mix lightly. Don't squeeze or manhandle it! Shape into patties slightly bigger then the buns they will be nestled in shortly, about 6 oz. each.

Pop them on a grill, or in a cast iron pan with sesame oil, or onto an indoor grill. However you cook them, just get them to about 160°F internally. Brush some melted butter or olive oil over the buns and toast them.

Throw all the slaw ingredients into a bowl and toss it to coat everything throughly.

Top the burgers with the slaw and serve. Feel free to drizzle burger with additional hoisin sauce before topping with slaw.

BOURBON BACON BURGER

Does it get any better than these 3 B's???

Bourbon is awesome to cook with. The natural smokiness adds a lot of depth to food across the board, from deserts to... well... burgers. Take it further by slathering it in our Bourbon Bacon Jam (pg. 25).

INGREDIENTS

BOURBON GLAZE

- 3 Tablespoons butter
- 2 small sweet onions, sliced thin
- 2 Tablespoons brown sugar
- ¼ teaspoon chili powder
- ½ teaspoon cumin
- ½ teaspoon salt
- 4 Tablespoons bourbon

BURGERS

- 12 strips of thick cut bacon
- 2 lbs. ground chuck (20% fat)
- 3 Tablespoons bourbon
- 1 ½ Tablespoons Worcestershire sauce
- 1 ½ teaspoons ground cumin
- 1 ½ teaspoons chili powder
- 1 ½ teaspoons salt
- 1 teaspoon pepper

Aged cheddar pairs extremely well with bourbon. If you can find an aged smoked yellow cheddar.... you are in for a delicious ride!

Lay the strips of bacon on a foil lined sheet tray. Place in COLD oven and kick the oven on to 400°F. Once the oven indicates it has hit that temperature, set a timer for 10 minutes. After 10 minutes, check the bacon. You are looking for "just about done". You don't want it super crispy where it breaks apart if it bends. If it's not there yet, just give it a few more minutes. Once it's ready, pull the sheet tray from the oven and remove bacon to paper towel lined plates. Don't you DARE dump that grease! Pour it through cheesecloth or a fine mesh strainer into a clean bowl or jar and pop that in the fridge. Use bacon grease to sauté anything. In the BC Kitchens, it's called Liquid Gold. It'll last a long time as long as the container is air tight.

MAKE THE BOURBON GLAZE: In a skillet over medium heat, melt the 3 Tablespoons of butter. Add the onions and cook for 10 minutes, stirring frequently until softened. Add the rest of the glaze ingredients and cook, stirring occasionally till the sauce thickens slightly, about 15 minutes. Remove from heat and let cool slightly.

While the glaze cooks, throw all the burger ingredients into a bowl and gently mix with your hands till combined. Don't squeeze or press into the meat. You'll end up with meatloaf burgers. Gently form meat into (4) 8oz. thick ass patties or (8) 4oz. smashable patties.

Cook the burgers in your preferred way till desired doneness. Gill over medium heat. Smash on a flattop. Cook in cast iron. Sizzle by flamethrower. *Burger Build:* bun, cheese (if adding), burger, bourbon glaze, bacon, bun top.

THE CHUTHOR BURGER

In honor of one of our biggest and bestest fans

Originally created (but not the same name... duh, lawsuits!) at a heavy metal themed burger chain, it was removed from their menu, much to the dismay of one of our dearest fans. So with a little research, we brought it back bigger and better for him! By selecting uncured versions of the meats used, we diffused the nitrate bomb that was the restaurants version.

INGREDIENTS

- 1 ½ lbs. ground sirloin
- 8 slices thick cut bacon
- 4 slices uncured Canadian bacon
- 4 thick slices uncured pancetta
- Red Onion Jam (pg. 25)
- Bacon Jam (pg. 25)
- 4 pretzel buns

DIRECTIONS

If you haven't already, craft a batch of the Red Onion Jam and the Bacon Jam. As they cool, move on to the meats.

Start by kicking on the grill, the flat top, the skillet on the stove... whatever cooking method you are using... to medium high heat. Form the beef into (4) 6oz. patties, about 20% larger than the buns they will be served in (shrinkage will occur during cooking... and there is nothing worse than a 7" bun with a 5" patty in it). Cut the pancetta and Canadian bacon into about ⅛" thick slices, as you probably bought these in their uncut forms.

GRILL: Set a cast iron pan on the grates for the meats and start cooking those bad boys. You want "near done" for the bacons and pancetta. Remove and drain on paper towel lined plates. Grill the burgers to desired doneness. Quickly butter the pretzel buns and pop them on the hot grates till toasted. Assemble.

SKILLET/FLATTOP: Place the bacons and pancetta on a foil lined sheet tray. Place in COLD oven and kick the oven on to 400°F. Once the oven indicates it has hit that temperature, check on them. Depending on how thick you sliced the pancetta and Canadian bacon, they may be done. If not, wait 10 minutes and check again. Don't cook until crispy... you want them to the point where you look at them and go "Ehhhh, almost done". Pop the burger patties in the skillet or on the flattop and cook till desired doneness. Assemble.

BURGER BUILD: Bottom pretzel bun, onion jam, bacon, burger patty, Canadian bacon, Bacon Jam, pancetta, top bun.

THE SCIENCE OF UMAMI
AKA: The Dynamics of the Droolz

The thought of a 6oz. fresh ground burger stacked with sautéed mushrooms, tomatoes, bacon, cheese, and ketchup with a side of fries is enough to make most of us start to drool. Why? *Umami.* Categorized as the "fifth" taste bud, alongside sweet, salty, bitter, and sour, umami is a taste profile that locks into the savory flavors. That burger I described above... every one of those ingredients are jam packed with an amino acid known as glutamate, and when you ingest something with high levels of glutamate, the compound binds itself to your taste bud receptors. In turn, your body creates more saliva and digestive juices, thus "drooling". When you process food by curing, aging, or fermenting, the free glutamates result in a stronger umami flavor. This is because the curing or fermenting process breaks down basic glutamate into free glutamate. You can thank Japanese chemist Kikunae Ikeda, who in 1908, isolated brown crystals of glutamic acid from defatted soybeans. He is also responsible for the concept of umami and placed it alongside the other 4 taste receptors.

Umami means "Essence of Deliciousness" in Japanese.

Now that you understand the basics of umami and glutamate, we need to address the savory elephant in the room: Monosodium Glutamate, or as the world knows it by... **MSG** *(also invented by Kikunae Ikeda)*. Now before you start throwing holy water on this book, know that the news, racism, and generations of people without access to the internet have been lying to you about MSG. It's not the evil horrible world ending additive that everyone made it out to be for decades. It was actually racism that did that. When Asian immigrants began settling in the U.S., they started opening food based businesses alongside Americans.

So, Americans did what they do best... invented rumors about the evils of MSG, claiming it caused dizziness, severe headaches, feelings of discomfort, etc. Anti-Communism sentiment was prevalent in the U.S. at this time, and in 1968, it was dubbed "Chinese Restaurant Syndrome"... because if you are going to destroy a whole nationality, go big or go home, right? The controversy around MSG is literally linked to xenophobia and racism against Chinese culture. Why? MSG was widely and openly used in processed foods being made in America as early as 1940, as well as being used in American owned restaurants. At this time, over 58 million pounds of MSG was being produced ***IN AMERICA*** and added to products by companies like Cambell's and Swanson, but faced absolutely no backlash. In a nutshell, the generation screaming the evils of MSG and responsible for propagating the false rumors were consuming it daily in their TV dinners and cans of soup. Hell, it was a necessity in many cook books for great mac & cheese, fried chicken, and homemade ranch dressing. Companies just gave it a cute name. *(Ac'cent anyone???)*

MSG has been reported to cause discomfort, headaches, cancer, brain damage, heart problems, bla bla bla. The Supreme Court of Pakistan even banned the sale and import of what they lovingly refer to as "Chinese Salt". However, decades of blind tests and scientifically backed rulings by the FDA, World Health Organization, United Nations Food, the Agriculture Organization, and FASEB proved that to be false. Sure, one or two subjects noted symptoms like headaches or bloating out of the thousands tested, but who doesn't occasionally feel something after eating a certain thing. Hell, I eat a certain brand of Greek yogurt and I feel slightly bloated. I'm not going to start calling it "Lactobacillus delbrueckii syndrome" and try to drive Greek restaurants out of business. I love tzatziki!

Even the International Headache Society removed MSG from its list of causative factors.

MSG IS SAFE TO EAT!

Sure, if you're ingesting a half a pound of it daily it could be dangerous over a long enough timeline... but the same can be said about salt, sugar, booze, ice cream, etc. Speaking of salt, MSG is actually a lot lower in sodium content then salt, while enhancing flavors 2x's as much and reducing sodium intake by <u>as much as two-thirds</u>!!! So, it's perfect for low sodium or iodine free dietary restrictions!

When you see that "No MSG" sign on restaurant windows or in menus... guess what? That meal you are about to eat is LOADED with salt to make up for it.

Some big name professional chefs have started speaking out in favor of MSG, calling it the "not-so-secret" ingredient everyone should be using. It adds roundness and depth to a dish, especially savory ones.

Wanna see just how awesome MSG can be for your dishes? Scramble up 4 eggs with a bit of salt and pepper. Divide the eggs into 2 pans and add a pinch of MSG to one of the pans as it cooks.

You are welcome.

Here's the cold hard facts... our bodies treat glutamate the same exact way whether it comes from the foods we eat (tomatoes, mushrooms, tuna, etc) or added as a seasoning (MSG).

In 2016, on an episode of *Parts Unknown*, Anthony Bourdain said:

"I think MSG is good stuff... You know what causes Chinese Restaurant Syndrome? Racism."

Foods Rich in Natural Umami:
(mg of Umami per 100g)

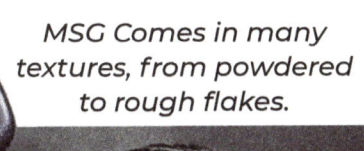

MSG Comes in many textures, from powdered to rough flakes.

Food	Umami (mg/100g)
Beef	10
Chicken	22
Potatoes	30-100
Corn	110
Broccoli	178
Tuna	188
Cheddar Cheese	190
Tomatoes	140-250
Dry-Cured Ham	340
Anchovies	630
Green Tea	220-670
Miso	200-700
Oyster Sauce	900
Dried Shiitake Mushrooms	1060
Roquefort Cheese	1280
Nori Seaweed	1378
Vegemite	1430
Parmesan Cheese	1680
Soy Sauce	400-1700
Marmite	1960

Kikunae Ikeda

GLUTAMIC ACID

A naturally occurring Amino Acid

GLUTAMATE

Deprotonated form of Glutamic Acid

MONOSODIUM GLUTAMATE

Sodium salt of Glutamic Acid

There is <u>NO CHEMICAL DIFFERENCE</u> between naturally occurring glutamate ions (like that found in seaweed and tomatoes) and the glutamate ions that make up MSG. Our bodies treat them exactly the same.

Think you've avoided MSG??? Think Again!

Any of these sound familiar???

- Monosodium Glutamate
- Monopotassium Glutamate
- Glutamate
- Glutamic Acid
- Hydrolyzed Protein
- Hydrolyzed Vegetable Protein
- Hydrolyzed Plant Protein
- Autolyzed Plant Protein
- Textured Protein
- Calcium Caseinate
- Sodium Caseinate
- Yeast Food
- Yeast Extract
- Yeast Nutrient
- Autolyzed Yeast
- Maltodextrins
- Hydrolyzed Oat Flour
- Malt Extract
- Malt Flavoring
- Malted Barley (flavor)
- Barley Malt
- Flavors or Flavoring(s)
- Natural Flavoring(s)
- Reaction Flavors
- Caramel Flavoring (coloring)
- Food Seasonings
- Bouillon

SIDES

Don't fret over side dishes. MOST will work with any dish without destroying the meal. But if you want to wow your guests with the perfect pairing to the main course, keep these 4 things in mind:

1 - _Flavor_ - Simple and flexible. You can stay within the flavor profile of your main dish by incorporating complimenting flavors into your side. Or keep the seasonal theme going through the entire meal. Or think opposites, and pair a savory main with an acidic side!

2 - _Weight_ - Heavy dishes with savory elements like meats and cheeses compliment perfectly with lighter sides.

3 - _Color_ - Sadly, we eat with our eyes first. Lighter colored dishes pair with similar sides. Pan seared salmon with a lemon cream sauce is great with a citrus rice side, but a pickled beet salad may throw guests off a bit (and if they won't eat it because of that, fuck um'. Throw their asses out).

4 - _Texture_ - Contrasting textures are a roller coaster for the mouth! Fried chicken, mashed potatoes, and a vinegar slaw salad are amazing examples of taste contrasting (savory + acidic) and texture contrasting (crispy + smooth + crunchy).

COOKING OILS & SMOKE POINTS
The goal is to NOT use the fire extinguisher!

Every oil available to use in a kitchen has 3 states: The Shimmer State, The Smoke Point, and The Flash Point. Smoke points are incredibly important to understand because they can make or break your cooking (and your kitchen if it ignites).

But what is a Smoke Point? It's the point where the oil starts breaking down due to high heat. Nutritional values, flavors, and benefits go kaput, and what happens instead are that free radicals start releasing into the food. One of these radicals, acrolein, is the chemical that adds a burnt, bitter, and disgusting taste to foods, along with having a strong aroma that causes watering eyes and that lingering smell you notice for about 2 weeks afterwards.

Once the oil starts smoking (not an instant concern, more on that later), you start getting near the Flash Point of the oil, meaning the oil is starting to off gas and can ignite over an open flame. And an open flame isn't always necessary. While experimenting for my oven baked chicken fingers, I misted virgin avocado oil (smoke point of about 400°F) on the tenders after breading and popped them in my electric oven at the broil setting, around 550°F. After 5 minutes, I checked on the tenders, and as soon as I opened the oven door, POOF! The tenders ignited. More shocked then freaked out, I pulled the sheet tray from the oven and popped them on the top of the stove. The flames extinguished pretty quickly on their own with little intervention from me, but it did reinforce the fact a fire extinguisher in the kitchen, **_MADE FOR THE KITCHEN_**, is important.

Smoking oil in a pan isn't a sign of impending ignition. If you are cooking in a wok, there's almost no way NOT to have oil smoking a bit since you are cooking at a ripping temperature. But in that scenario, you are cooking quickly, and the food being added will lower the temp of the oil on contact.

What's funny about oil is that when you hit the smoke point of an oil, you'll actually lower the smoke point of the oil during the next usage (mainly in the case of deep frying). That is why if you do a lot of deep frying, it's better to invest in an oil with a much higher smoke point then what you'll be frying at. Why? Because you'll want to get that oil to about 50°F hotter than what it needs to be to compensate the rapid drop in temperature when adding food. Since most foods cap off at 375°F for deep frying, a good corn or peanut oil is perfect, as their smoke points are around 450°F. Peanut is our go-to deep frying oil in the Bite Club Kitchens. In my opinion, fries always taste better coming out of peanut oil.

Water, heat, light and air, are the enemies of cooking oils. These will cause oil to become rancid, so don't store your oils over or even near the stove... the residual heat will speed up the decay of the oil, especially if they are flavored and lighter, like olive oil. Cool, dark storage with the cap tightly on will preserve the oil for a long while, and if the oil is in a clear glass or plastic bottle, wrap it in foil or another dark cloth to block out light.

THE SMOKE POINT LIST

I've compiled a list of the most common cooking oils, their (average) smoke points, whether they are neutral flavored or will impart their own flavor in cooking, and what methods of culinary madness they are best suited for. This list was compiled from numerous sources available on the internet, cooking manuals, culinary schools, and oil manufacturers. The smoke point temps. listed are averages, as the true smoke point may differ slightly depending on refining and processing techniques used by producers.

Oil	Smoke Point	Flavor	Uses
Flax Oil	225°F	Flavored	5
Walnut Oil	320°F	Flavored	5
EV Olive Oil	325-375°F	Flavored	1, 3, 5
Coconut Oil	350°F	Flavored	1, 2, 4
Sesame Oil	350-400°F	Flavored	1, 6
Butter	350°F	Flavored	1, 2+, 3, 4
Vegetable Shortening	360°F	Neutral	1, 3
Duck Fat	375°F	Neutral (kinda)	1, 2, 4
Chicken Fat (Schmaltz)	375°F	Flavored	1, 2, 3, 4, 5
Virgin Avocado Oil	375-400°F	Flavored	1, 2, 3, 4, 5
Lard	370°F	Flavored	1, 2, 3, 4, 7
Grapeseed Oil	390°F	Neutral	1, 2, 3, 4, 5
Canola Oil	400°F	Neutral	1, 2, 3, 4, 6, 7, 8, 9
Beef Tallow	400°F	Flavored	1, 2, 3, 4, 7
Vegetable Oil	400-450°F	Neutral	1, 2, 3, 4, 6, 7, 8, 9
Almond Oil	430°F	Flavored	1, 2, 4, 9
Sunflower Oil	440°F	Neutral	1, 2, 3, 4, 7, 8, 9
Corn Oil	450°F	Neutral	1, 2, 3, 4, 7, 8, 9
Clarified Butter (Ghee)	450°F	Flavored	1, 2, 3, 4
Peanut Oil	450°F	Neutral	1, 2, 3, 4, 6, 7, 8, 9
Soybean Oil	450°F	Neutral	1, 2, 3, 4, 7, 8, 9
Refined Olive Oil	425-465°F	Flavored	1, 2, 3, 4, 9
Rice Bran Oil	490°F	Neutral	1, 2, 3, 4, 5, 6, 7, 8, 9
Safflower Oil	510°F	Neutral	1, 2, 3, 4, 7, 8, 9
Avocado Oil	520°F	Flavored	1, 2, 3, 4, 5, 9

KEY

1= Sauté
2= Pan-Fry
2+= Quick Pan Fry
3= Baking
4= Roasting
5= Dressing/Marinades/Smoothies
6= Stir-frying
7= Deep-frying
8= Searing
9= Grilling

WARNING: NEVER USE WATER TO EXTINGUISH AN OIL FIRE!!! WATER JUST PISSES OFF THE OIL AND ACTS LIKE A GREMLIN: POPS AND SPREADS RAPIDLY. **TO EXTINGUISH AN OIL FIRE, YOU MUST SUFFOCATE IT.** USE AN APPROVED KITCHEN FIRE EXTINGUISHER OR DUMP FLOUR/CORNSTARCH/BAKING SODA OVER IT. IF IT HAPPENS IN A PAN ON THE STOVE TOP, COVER THE PAN WITH ITS LID.

FRENCH FRIES

Fries before... well, everything!

Fries are not bad for you, they are a vegetable. Dr. Social Media told me so!

FRIED

INGREDIENTS

- **6 large russet potatoes (plan on 2 medium potatoes per person)**
- **2 quarts vegetable oil, canola oil, or our preferred choice: peanut oil**

DIRECTIONS

Wash, dry, and slice the potatoes to ½" thick slices. If you happen to have a mandolin slicer, this will make it so much faster. Toss the potatoes into a bowl of ice cold water for at least an hour, or overnight. This step is crucial, as it pulls the starch from the potatoes. If soaking longer than an hour, store the bowl in the fridge. When ready to fry, rinse the sliced potatoes with cold water and lay on a dish towel. With another towel, pat the fries as dry as possible. Dry = Crispy!

Heat up the oil in a deep fryer or a deep pot to 300°F. You'll need a thermometer for this. Gently lower the potatoes into the oil and cook them in batches for 5-6 minutes. Don't overcrowd the pot. I know, they still look raw. What you did was "set the starch". You will be frying them at a higher temperature in a bit.

Remove the fries to a paper towel lined plate and kick up the heat on that oil to 400°F. Why so high? Because when you add the fries back in, the temp. will lower, so this is to compensate for that.

Again, gently lower the fries back into the oil and cook again, in batches, for about 5 minutes or until golden brown. Once cooked, return the fries to a paper towel lines plate and sprinkle on your seasoning. NOSH AWAY!!!

DON'T STOP AT JUST SALT! TRY SPRINKLING ON SOME OF YOUR FAVORITE RUBS OR SPICE MIXES. OR GRATED CHEESE LIKE PARMESAN. OR PRE-MADE FLAVOR PACKETS LIKE RANCH OR TACO SEASONING. RAMEN PACKETS ARE GREAT FOR THIS, AS THEY HAVE FLAVOR AND SALT!

BAKED

INGREDIENTS

- **6 large russet potatoes (plan on 2 medium potatoes per person)**
- **2 Tablespoons vegetable or canola oil**

DIRECTIONS

Follow the same directions as the FRIED side by washing, slicing, and soaking the potatoes in cold water. Kick on the oven to 450°F with a rack in the middle.

After soaking, pat the fries dry between dish towels. While drying, heat up enough water to cover the fries in a bowl; either by microwave or kettle or mutant ability. It doesn't need to be boiling, but it needs to be very hot.

Place the potatoes in a heat proof bowl and carefully pour the very hot water over them, covering them by at least an inch. Let sit for 10 minutes.

WHY??? You are basically blanching the potatoes and setting the starches, much like the lower temperature first frying. This will result in a crispier French fry from the oven.

After 10 minutes, remove the potatoes from the hot water to another set of dish towels. Dump the hot water out of the bowl and wipe dry. Gently pat the potatoes dry and return to the bowl. Drizzle the oil over the fries and toss with your hands till each piece is coated with oil.

Lay the potatoes out in a single layer on a sheet tray brushed with a bit of oil. Bake the potatoes for 15-20 minutes. Remove the sheet tray, and with a spatula, flip the fries. Return to the oven for another 10 minutes or until it hits your desired crispiness. Remove from oven, sprinkle with whatever the hell you want, and nosh away!

LOADED TOTS
A meal in itself

If you don't have a cast iron pan in the house, this is the reason to get one. By preheating it in the oven, you are insured crispy on the outside, smooth on the inside tots. We will give you the Bite Club version of how to load this up, but it's totally up to your imagination!

INGREDIENTS

- 1 lb. frozen tater tots
- 1 lb. ground sirloin (min 90/10)
- 1 ½ Tablespoons hot sauce, chili sauce or Buffalo sauce
- 2 teaspoons salt
- 2 teaspoons chili powder
- 1 teaspoon ground cumin
- 2 teaspoons garlic
- 1 ½ teaspoons paprika
- 2-4 Cups shredded cheese (Mexican, cheddar, pepper jack, etc., and if possible, freshly grated)
- red onion, diced
- diced tomatoes
- sour cream
- minced cilantro (optional)

To make this vegetarian, leave meat out completely or replace it with meatless crumbles or Buffalo marinated cooked tofu.

DIRECTIONS

Kick the oven on to 425°F. If you have a cast iron skillet, toss that in there as it heats up. If you do not have one, it's ok. But get one. Seriously. They are awesome.

When the oven reaches temperature, CAREFULLY grab the skillet from the oven and dump in the tater tots. There will be a pile. If you do not have cast iron, spread tater tots out on a baking dish or in a pie plate.

Bake the tots for 20 minutes. If using cast iron, carefully give the tots a flip to move the top ones to the bottom half way through cooking. Remove from oven and set aside. Lower the oven temp to 375°F.

Back on the stovetop, heat a skillet over medium heat. Add a drizzle of oil to the pan and then add the ground beef, hot sauce, and all the spices. Make sure to break up beef with a spatula and stir until beef is fully cooked, around 5 minutes. Remove from heat.

If using cast iron, remove half the tots. Top with half of the beef. Sprinkle a layer of cheese. Repeat layering of tater tots, beef, and cheese. Otherwise, place a layer of tots in a baking dish, then top with half of the beef. Sprinkle a layer of cheese. Repeat layering of tater tots, beef, and cheese.

Place in oven and bake for 5–7 minutes, until cheese is all gooey.

Remove from oven and top with the rest of the ingredients. Grab a fork and dig in!

MAQUE CHOUX

A side dish you will probably just eat as a meal!

Corn off the cob or canned corn for those in a rush, this NOLA inspired dish is packed with flavor and spice. Customize the heat levels by supplementing some of the red peppers with hotter ones. You can replace the heavy cream with chicken stock for a more traditional style, but we find the cream not only manages the heat a little better, but adds a very savory and smooth texture to the dish.

INGREDIENTS

- 5-6 slices of raw bacon, chopped
- 3 Cups corn (about 4 ears or 2 cans. If using canned, drain corn first)
- 1 yellow onion, diced
- 2 jalapeño peppers, diced
- 1 red bell pepper, diced
- 1-2 Tablespoons Cajun seasoning
- ½ Cup heavy cream

DIRECTIONS

Get a large skillet going over medium heat. Toss the chopped bacon in and cook till crispy, around 8 minutes. Do not get rid of the bacon grease. Stir in the onion, peppers, and Cajun seasoning. Cook for around 10 more minutes until most of the liquids from the veggies have disappeared and the onions and peppers are soft.

Add the heavy cream (or chicken stock) and stir for about 2-3 minutes. If using cream, it should thicken slightly. Serve!

CAJUN SEASONING RECIPE

THIS SPICE RUB IS SUPER SIMPLE TO TOSS TOGETHER WITH INGREDIENTS YOU PROBABLY HAVE SITTING IN YOUR CABINETS. PLUS, YOU CONTROL WHAT GOES IN IT! DON'T WANT IT SPICY? REDUCE THE PEPPER AMOUNTS! OR ADD MORE IF YOU WANT IT TO BURN! GREAT ON ALMOST ANYTHING, FROM CHICKEN TO FRENCH FRIES! STORES FOR MONTHS IN AN AIR TIGHT CONTAINER.

- 3 Tablespoons paprika (smoked if possible)
- 2 Tablespoons Kosher or sea salt
- 2 Tablespoons garlic powder
- 1 Tablespoon onion powder
- 1 Tablespoon ground black pepper
- 1 Tablespoon ground white pepper
- 1 Tablespoon cayenne (halve if you don't want it to be too hot, or add more if you want it spicy)
- 1 Tablespoon dried oregano
- ½ Tablespoon dried thyme

Toss all ingredients in a mason jar or air tight container and give it a good shake to mix it all up.

CUCUMBER SALAD

Tangy, refreshing... just perfection

If there was any side dish I could eat forever, it would be a cucumber salad. English cucumbers are the star of the show here, and with the tang of seasoned rice vinegar (store-bought or up the ante and make it yourself), this refreshing salad is filling, healthy, and amazing any time of the year.

INGREDIENTS

- **2 large English cucumbers, halved and sliced thin (or quartered and sliced thicker)**
- **1 teaspoon salt**
- **¼ red onion, sliced thin**
- **¼ Cup rice vinegar**

DIRECTIONS

Place cucumbers in a strainer and toss with the salt to help them release water. Let this sit for about 15 minutes. Do not rinse the cucumbers.

Place in a bowl and toss with remaining ingredients. Taste and adjust vinegar and salt. Serve or chill till ready.

ASIAN CUCUMBER SALAD

Add to the above recipe:

- **2 teaspoons ginger, grated or 1 teaspoon powdered ginger**
- **2 cloves garlic, finely minced**
- **1 Tablespoon soy sauce**
- **1 Tablespoon toasted sesame oil**
- **1 Tablespoon honey**
- **1-2 teaspoons sriracha**
- **1–2 Tablespoons toasted sesame seeds**

Toss and Serve.

GREEK CUCUMBER SALAD

EXCLUDE RICE VINEGAR

Add to the above recipe:

- **4-6 Roma tomatoes, chopped**
- **¼ Cup good olive oil**
- **1 ½ Tablespoons lemon juice**
- **2 teaspoons dried oregano**
- **¾ Cup crumbled feta cheese**
- **black olives, pitted and sliced**
- **salt and pepper, to taste**

Toss and Serve.

WATERMELON CUCUMBER SALAD

EXCLUDE RICE VINEGAR

Add to the above recipe:

- **1 Tablespoon olive oil**
- **¼ teaspoon salt**
- **1 Tablespoon fresh lemon juice**
- **2 Cups cubed seedless watermelon**
- **1 Tablespoon thinly sliced fresh basil**

Toss and Serve.

The base recipe above is a perfect start to really get creative with this salad. Add chilled shrimp, or diced celery for an epic crunch. Try different seasonings! This was MADE for a good furikake seasoning. Add diced tomatoes and crispy bacon for a BLT inspired salad. Toss in sliced radishes or daikon. Splash with some saké. Have fun and make it your own!

Pico De Galo

AKA Salsa Fresca, AKA Fresh Salsa, AKA Damn Yummy

Like a perfect salsa without all the excess liquid, Pico De Galo is made for chip dipping, but there's so much more! Pile it in your tacos! Top a grilled chicken breast. Add it to queso! Mix it into a frittata or omelets! Top that quesadilla! Or just sprinkle it on your salad!

INGREDIENTS

- **6 Roma tomatoes, diced, excess liquid discarded**
- **½ Cup yellow onion, chopped**
- **1 -2 jalapeño peppers, seeded, and minced**
- **4 Tablespoons chopped fresh cilantro**
- **1 teaspoon cumin**
- **3 Tablespoons lime juice**
- **1 teaspoon salt**
- **dash of pepper**

Toss all in a bowl and gently mix together. Adjust salt and lime juice to your liking.

Pico De Customization!

- Replace the jalapeño with any pepper. Red peppers for the lightest of heat or crank it to habaneros. Hell, even ghost peppers if you can get them fresh!

- Add 2 diced avocados and ½ Cup crumbled cotija cheese. Adjust salt and lime juice to your liking.

- Try adding 1 ½ lbs. of grilled pineapple (diced) to the pico for a sweet summer taste.

- Try mixing up your peppers. Poblanos and Fresno chilies work wonderfully with the jalapeño.

- If you are not a fan of cilantro, replace with flat leaf Italian parsley.

- Turn the pico into a great bruschetta topping by losing the peppers and adding fresh basil with a heavy splash of red wine vinegar.

- Replace a third of the lime juice with your favorite tequila for a grown up pico!

- Add a squirt of sriracha for a new kind of kick (add before tossing in the salt, as sriracha is pretty salty).

GUACA-HOLY-MOLE

The most overcharged add-on ever!

Save yourself the $2 bucks for a sad teaspoon of the stuff on your burrito bowl and make it yourself!

CHUNKY STYLE

INGREDIENTS

- 2 large ripe avocados
- 2 Tablespoons lime juice
- 3 Roma tomatoes, chopped, juice discarded
- 1 medium onion, diced
- ½ teaspoon salt
- 2 garlic cloves, minced
- ½ teaspoon ground cumin
- ⅛ teaspoon cayenne pepper

DIRECTIONS

Peel, pit, and mash the avocados with the lime juice. A fork works well, or grab that potato masher and go to work on it. Once mashed, mix in the rest of the ingredients until well incorporated. Store in an airtight container.

CREAMY STYLE

INGREDIENTS

- 2 large ripe avocados
- ½ Cup sour cream
- ¼ Cup Pico De Gallo (oh look, a recipe on the previous page!)
- ½ Tablespoon taco seasoning
- 2 Tablespoons lime juice
- 1 Tablespoon cumin
- ½ teaspoon salt (or more to taste)

DIRECTIONS

Peel, pit, and mash the avocados with a fork, or if you want a really creamy guac, pulse the avocados in a food processor till smooth.

Add remaining ingredients and mix/pulse until smooth and well combined.

Transfer to an airtight container. Refrigerate for at least an hour before enjoying. This gives the guacamole time to meld and develop deep flavors.

You can really play with the spices here. Add more cumin or red pepper. Or try a spicy taco seasoning. If you find the texture of either style too thick, thin it out with a bit more lime juice... or tequila! But go slow. It's easier to thin it out then to have to thicken it back up without really altering the flavor.

TACO SEASONING MIX

1 Tablespoon chili powder • 1 Tablespoon cumin
½ teaspoon paprika • ½ teaspoon onion powder
¼ garlic powder • ⅛ teaspoon red pepper
½ teaspoon salt • 1 teaspoon pepper

HUMMUS - 5 WAYS

Hummina Hummina Hummus!

The crazy good dip that turns a veggie tray into Fancy AF Crudités

CLASSIC

- 30 oz. canned chickpeas drained, liquid reserved
- ½ Cup tahini
- ¼ Cup olive oil
- 4 Tablespoons lemon juice
- 3 garlic cloves
- 2 Tablespoons cumin
- 1 Tablespoon paprika (preferably smoked)
- 2 teaspoon salt

BLACK BEAN

- 1 (15 oz.) can black beans, drained (liquid reserved) and rinsed
- ¼ Cup chopped fresh cilantro
- 2 Tablespoons tahini
- 2 Tablespoons fresh lime juice
- 2 Tablespoons reserved black bean liquid
- 1 Tablespoon extra-virgin olive oil
- 1 ½ teaspoons ground cumin
- ¼ teaspoon salt
- 2 garlic cloves, peeled
- ½ small jalapeño pepper, seeded

CHOCOLATE

Cause why not have a dessert hummus?!?

- 15 oz. can of chickpeas drained
- ¼ Cup peanut butter
- 4 Tablespoons milk
- ¾ Cup mini chocolate chips
- 4 Tablespoons maple syrup
- ¼ Cup cocoa powder
- 2 teaspoons espresso powder
- ½ teaspoon cinnamon
- 2 teaspoons vanilla extract
- ½ teaspoon salt

FREAKY PUMPKIN

Serve this in a hollowed-out half of a small pumpkin!

- 15 oz. can of chickpeas drained, liquid reserved
- 15 oz. pumpkin puree
- 3 Tablespoons tahini
- 1 ½ Tablespoons olive oil
- 2 Tablespoons lemon juice
- 2 cloves garlic
- 1 teaspoon salt
- 2 teaspoons cumin
- 1 ½ teaspoons pumpkin pie spice

SMOOTH AVOCADO

- 15 oz. can of chickpeas drained, liquid reserved
- 2 ripe avocados, peeled and pitted
- 3 cloves garlic minced
- 2 Tablespoons tahini
- 1 lime juiced
- ½ teaspoon salt
- 2 teaspoons cumin
- 1 teaspoon paprika
- ½ teaspoon ground coriander

DIRECTIONS

For all hummus EXCEPT chocolate:
Place all ingredients into a food processor or blender and pulse until smooth. If hummus is too thick, thin it by adding more of the reserved bean liquid.

For Chocolate Dessert Hummus:
Place all ingredients EXCEPT chickpeas in a food processor or blender and blend until combined. Add in chickpeas and blend until smooth. If too thick, add in small amounts of milk and pulse until desired consistency. Serve with pretzels and graham crackers.

SMOKEY CAMPFIRE BBQ BEANS

I literally cannot show up to a party without these...

Seriously... I'm starting to think I was only invited to parties because of these! Smokey flavors, sweet sauces, savory bacon, and chunks of ham come together for this rich side.

INGREDIENTS

- 2 cans (15 oz. each) of pork and beans
- 2 Cans (15 oz. each) of black beans, rinsed and drained
- 2 Cans (15 oz. each) of red kidney beans, rinsed and drained
- 1 lb of thick cut smoked bacon, cooked and chopped
- 1 lb of smoked ham, diced

- 2 large bell peppers, color your choice, diced
- 1-2 jalapeños, deseeded and diced
- 2 large yellow or sweet onions, rough diced
- 2 Cups of your favorite BBQ sauce
- 2 Cups of brown sugar
- 6 cloves garlic, minced

NOTE: THIS MAKES ENOUGH FOR 10-15 PEOPLE. FEEL FREE TO HALVE IT OR TRIPLE IT TO ACCOMMODATE YOUR NEEDS. IT SCALES BEAUTIFULLY!

Slow Cooker Directions

If you haven't already, cook and dice the bacon. Toss all the ingredients into the slow cooker and cook on low for 8-9 hours, or on high for 4-5 hours. Stir every hour or so. Halfway through cooking, tilt/offset the lid of the slow cooker to allow steam to escape and thicken the beans. If the mixture is too thick for your liking, stir in more of your favorite BBQ sauce.

Stovetop / Fire Pit Directions

Cast iron is going to be the best option here. Toss all ingredients into the pot over med heat (for the stovetop) or hot indirect heat (on top of the coals in the fire pit). You'll have to stir more often to prevent the sugars from burning too quickly. Cook 2-3 hours until veggies are soft yet still give off a bit of crunch. Offset lid halfway through cooking to steam off liquids.

TOO THIN??? HOW?

You have vegetables giving off water. If you bought pre-diced ham, that could have been packed in a water solution. Your favorite bbq sauce may be using water as a filler. You never know how much water veggies can be holding. Hell, a raw red bell pepper is 94% water!!! Offsetting the lid halfway through cooking helps steam off the excess liquid, but sometimes you need a bit more help.

Mix 2 Tablespoons of cornstarch with 2 Tablespoons cold water and whisk till smooth. Dump into beans and stir till incorporated. Repeat if necessary, but don't be too anxious. Time is your friend here. Sometimes waiting those few extra minutes will get you the desired results.

QUICKIE GARLIC BREADSTICKS

Soft on the inside, warm on the soul...

These monsters come together quickly and require almost no rise time. I know, weird for a dough recipe, huh? This happened from a mix-up between two dough batches, one that had been rising for hours and another that went on to rise for a fraction of the time. If you like that one franchise's version with their unlimited soup and salad, you'll love these!

INGREDIENTS

- 1 ½ Cups very warm water (100°F-110°F)
- 1 packet instant yeast (2 ½ teaspoons)
- 2 Tablespoons sugar
- 1 Tablespoon olive oil
- 3-4 Cups flour + more for kneading
- 1 Tablespoon Kosher salt
- 6 Tablespoons butter, melted (if using unsalted butter, stir in ½ teaspoon of salt after melting)
- 1 Tablespoon garlic powder

In a large bowl, stir the water, sugar, and yeast together. Let sit for 10 minutes. It should get all nice and foamy. Once foamy, stir in 2 Cups of the flour and the olive oil.

Gradually mix in more flour (1-2 Cups) and the salt until you have a soft, shaggy dough.

With flour-dusted hands, transfer the dough to a floured surface and knead for 2-3 minutes. You may need to mix in more flour until a smooth ball of dough is achieved.

Place the dough in a greased bowl, cover with a towel, and allow to rise for 30 minutes in a warm place.

Kick that oven on to 400°F. Divide dough in half. Then divide those in half. Repeat till you have 12-16 parts (the less number of dough balls, the bigger the breadsticks will be).

Roll each into a log about 8-10 inches long and place 2-inches apart on a greased baking sheet. If you have silicone baking mats, give them a spritz of nonstick spray before placing dough on them.

Bake the dough for 5 minutes. Melt the butter in the microwave and mix in the garlic powder.

After 5 minutes, gently brush the breadsticks with the garlic butter and continue to bake for another 6-8 minutes. You want them golden. Remove from oven when they are "just about" done. They will continue to bake on the sheet pan as they rest. Brush with remaining garlic butter and dig in!

CUSTOMIZE THIS!!!!

Why stop with garlic powder? Add a Tablespoon of Italian seasoning. Or omit the garlic and replace with a hearty sprinkling of everything bagel seasoning. Or pizza seasoning! Sprinkle on some parmesan. Or top with fresh shredded cheese and bake!

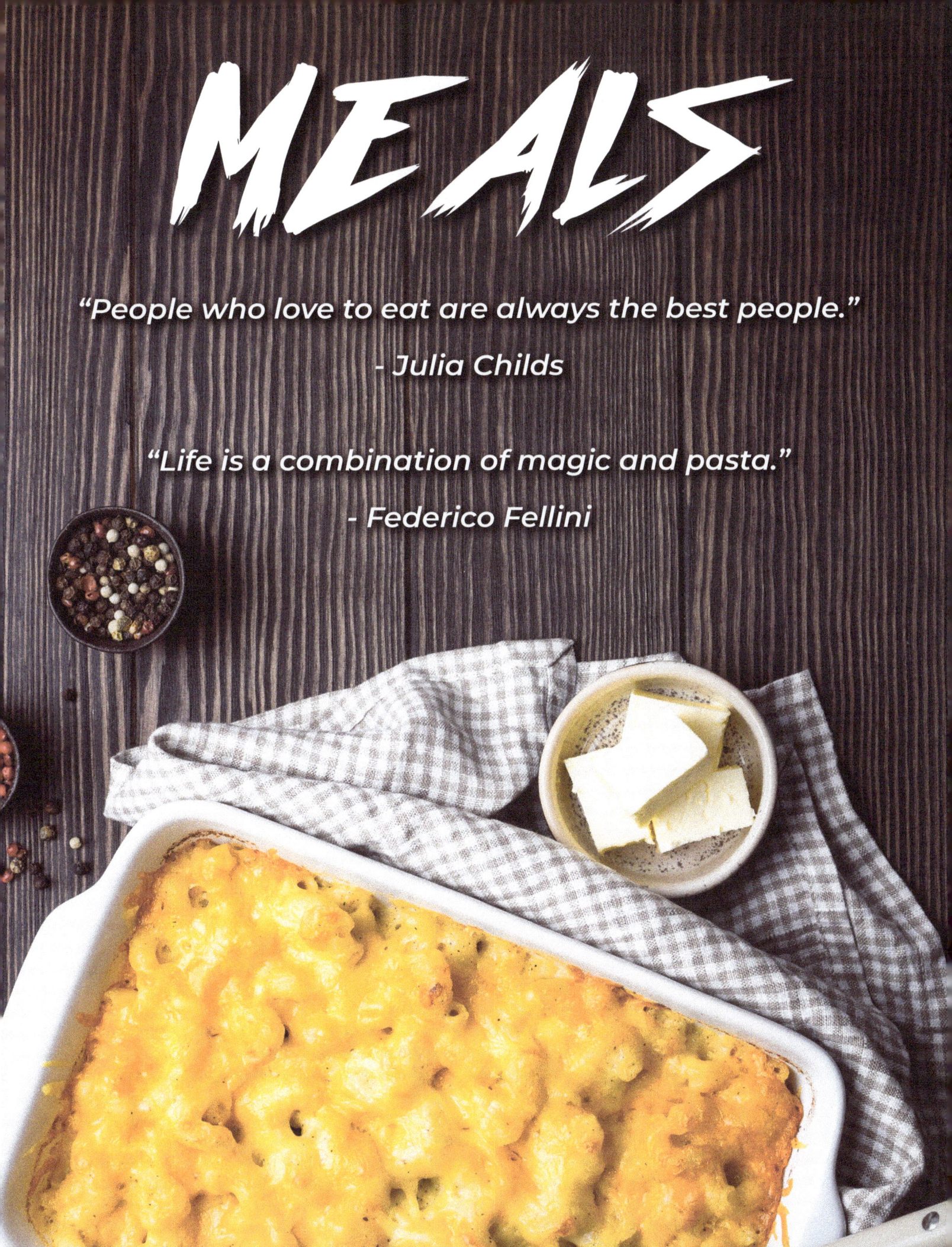

MEALS

"People who love to eat are always the best people."

- Julia Childs

"Life is a combination of magic and pasta."

- Federico Fellini

BUFFALO CHICKEN MAC & CHEESE

Hot Damn... this is so good!

Taking the love of wings to a whole new savory level.

INGREDIENTS

- 16 oz. dry cavatappi noods
- 6 Tablespoons butter
- 6 Tablespoons flour
- 1 teaspoon garlic powder
- 1 teaspoon onion powder
- 2 Cups whole milk
- 1 Cup heavy cream
- 1 teaspoon dry mustard powder
- salt to taste
- 2 ½ Cups cheddar, shredded
- 2 Cups pepper jack, shredded
- ⅔ - 1 Cup buffalo sauce
- 1 lb. diced/shredded cooked chicken
- 1 Cup panko bread crumbs
- 3 Tablespoons butter melted

DIRECTIONS

Drop the dry noodles into a boiling pot of salted water and cook for 2 minutes less than what the package suggests. You want them to be a bit denser then al denté. Once cooked, drain and rinse under cold water. We need to stop the cooking process. Don't worry, the noods will continue to cook in the oven.

Kick the oven on to 400°F. Grab a large sauce pan and melt the butter over medium heat. Whisk in the flour, garlic, and onion powders. Keep whisking until it's almost ball of smoothness, about 1-2 minutes.

Start adding the milk and heavy cream, ½ Cup at a time, whisking constantly. Then add in the dry mustard powder and whisk till incorporated. Bring the mixture to a boil. Keep whisking! Boil the mixture for 1 minute.

While it boils, combine the noods and chicken in a large bowl.

Once the milk mixture has boiled for a minute, kill the heat and start adding in the cheeses by the handful, whisking each time until smooth. After all the cheese has been added, dump in the buffalo sauce. Whisk a bit more, then dump the cheese mixture into the bowl over the noods and chicken. Fold together with a spatula. Taste. Add salt if needed (some buffalo sauces are saltier then others).

Spray or grease a 9"x13" pan, then dump in the mixture, spreading it evenly. In a bowl, combine the melted butter and panko, then spread over the cheesy noods.

Bake for 20-25 minutes. You want the cheese to be bubbling and the topping to be a toasty brown. Serve hot!

For those who actually like it, top with crumbled bleu cheese.

Although sharp cheddar is the standard go-to for mac & cheese, feel free to mix it up! At Bite Club, we like equal parts of mild cheddar, sharp cheddar, and pepper jack. Gruyere is also wonderful, along with gouda, muenster, fontina, Monterey jack, and havarti. You can even use brie... just make sure to pop off the rind!

OOEY GOOEY CREAMY MAC & CHEESE

Childhood classic for the adult kid!

Ditch the elbow macaroni and grab some ridged cavatappi noodles. This quick and easy throw together is kid friendly and the perfect comfort food.

INGREDIENTS

- **1 lb. cavatappi noodles, uncooked**
- **4 Tablespoons butter**
- **4 Tablespoons flour**
- **1 teaspoon sea salt**
- **1 Tablespoon powdered mustard**
- **2 teaspoons garlic powder**
- **1 teaspoon paprika**
- **1 Cup half & half**
- **1 ½ Cups whole milk**
- **4 Cups shredded cheese (*see notes)**
- **4 oz. cream cheese, cubed**
- **fresh ground pepper**

DIRECTIONS

Get a pot of water boiling for the noods. Add in at least 2 Tablespoons of salt to the water before adding the noodles. Cook until al dente, drain, and set aside. DO NOT RINSE NOODLES!

In a medium saucepan over medium-high heat, melt the butter. When it starts to foam, sprinkle in the flower and stir until the mixture becomes thick and pasty, about a minute. Whisk in the milk and half & half and bring to a simmer. Stir often until mixture thickens, about 5 minutes.

Start adding cheeses by the handful, stirring after each addition. The cheese will melt fast. Stir in the salt, garlic powder, powdered mustard, and paprika, then fold in the cream cheese cubes and stir until melted. Mix in the cooked pasta and serve warm.

Look, that bag of pre-shredded cheese is an easy grab, but to get the utmost gooeyest results for mac and cheese, pizza, taco bakes, lasagna... really anything that requires a layer of cheese, you need to buy a block of cheese and shred it yourself. We dive into the facts of "Pre-Shredded Cheese" deeper on the next spread.

PIZZA DOUGH!!

Do good. Be nice. Eat Pizza. Repeat.

Our dough is a delightful hybrid between Chicago style and New York style. Chewy, foldable, and so versatile! Pizza, calzones, flatbread, dough knots, stromboli, pot-pie toppers... this pizza dough will deliver on texture and taste.

INGREDIENTS

- **1 ½ Cups warm water, about 100°F-105°F**
- **1 Tablespoon active dry yeast**
- **2 teaspoons sugar**
- **1 Tablespoon olive oil**
- **4+ Cups all-purpose or (strongly recommend) 00' flour**
- **2 teaspoons fine sea salt**

2 HOUR DOUGH:

Place dough back into bowl, then into the oven with the light on. Boil a small pan of water, and once it begins boiling, place the pan of water in the oven. Keep the door closed for 2 hours.

6-8 HOUR DOUGH:

Place dough back into proofing bowl, cover with plastic wrap, and place in a draft free spot in the kitchen. At the 4-hour mark, punch the dough down. That will let it know who's boss. Remove dough and continue with recipe.

24 HOUR DOUGH:

This will give you the most well-rounded flavor of the dough. Place the dough in the bowl or container that is triple the size of the dough, then cover and place in fridge. After 24 hours, remove and let sit on counter for 2 hours before rolling out.

DIRECTIONS

Take a steel mixing bowl, or the bowl of your mixer, turn it upside down and run it under warm water. This will help stabilize the temperature. Make sure not to get the inside of the bowl wet. Dry it off and mix the water and sugar in the bowl. Sprinkle the yeast over the top, give it a quick stir, and let it sit for 10 minutes. It should be foamy. Pour in the oil and stir again. Now start mixing in the flour, a Cup at a time (on low speed with dough hook if using a mixer). After the third Cup of flour, you want to add it in using smaller amounts. What you are looking for is a bit shaggy, mostly smooth dough with no dry spots and just a bit sticky to the touch. Cover dough with a damp towel and place somewhere warm (inside the oven with the oven light on creates a perfect proofing spot). Let rest for about 30-35 minutes. Remove, sprinkle on the salt, and knead just until incorporated.

From here, see proofing times to finish your dough.

Once proofed, flour your surface and roll the dough out to desired shape and thickness. If the dough pulls back from its shape, let it rest 15 minutes and try again. This allows the gluten to chill TF out and become relaxed.

Preheat oven with the pizza stone on the upper 1/3 rack to as hot as it can go (usually 500°F-550°F). Place dough on a well-floured pizza peel, or you can use the back of a sheet pan (also well-floured). You are going to make a mess... deal with it. Top pizza with desired ingredients, then slide the pizza onto the pizza stone. Bake for 6-8 minutes, keeping an eye on the dough to make sure it doesn't burn. Remove, let cool for a few minutes, then slice and nosh!

THE IMPORTANCE OF A PIZZA STONE...

Splurge for a rectangle one as big as your oven can hold. Round ones are ok... but you are limited to only 1 pizza at a time. Also, keep it in your oven at all times on the bottom rack. It'll act as an amazing heat sink and keep your oven at a more stable temperature, helping minimize hot spots. And if it gets too dirty, just run the oven cleaning cycle with it inside. It'll come out looking almost brand new!

BITE CLUB'S PIZZA SAUCE!

- 28-32 oz. can crushed tomatoes - San Marzano if you wish
- 2 teaspoons garlic powder
- 1 teaspoon onion powder
- 1 Tablespoon dried oregano
- ½ teaspoon dried thyme
- 1 teaspoon dried parsley
- 1 teaspoon black pepper
- 1 teaspoon Kosher salt
- 2 Tablespoons minced fresh basil
- 2 teaspoons sugar
- splash extra virgin olive oil
- splash of balsamic vinegar

POP ALL THE INGREDIENTS EXCEPT THE SUGAR, OIL, AND VINEGAR INTO A SAUCEPAN OVER LOW HEAT AND SIMMER FOR 20 MINUTES, STIRRING OCCASIONALLY. TASTE. IF USING SAN MARZANO CRUSHED TOMATOES, YOU MAY NOT NEED TO ADD THE SUGAR, AS THEIR NATURAL SWEETNESS WILL BALANCE THE SAUCE. BUT IF YOU FIND THE SAUCE NEEDS THAT SWEET BOOST, ADD IN THE SUGAR, A TEASPOON AT A TIME. ONCE IT'S TO YOUR LIKING, STIR IN THE FRESH BASIL, AND GIVE IT A SPLASH OF OIL AND THE VINEGAR. SIMMER 5 MORE MINUTES.

ALLOW TO COOL TO ROOM TEMPERATURE BEFORE TOPPING YOUR PIZZA. CAN BE MADE AHEAD OF TIME AND STORED IN AN AIR TIGHT CONTAINER FOR UP TO 3 DAYS, OR FROZEN FOR 6 MONTHS.

The Cheesy Facts

There's a good chance you just spent well over 24 hours making the dough (and trust me when I say you are going to want to make the 24-hour dough), and now you are gonna top it with pre-shredded generic cheese?

Pre-shredded cheese is an easy go to, but the truth is, that stuff is coated with anti-coagulation ingredients like potato starches, cornstarch, calcium sulfate (the same stuff used to make cement and floor tiles), and cellulose (aka non-digestible vegetable fiber) that keeps it from clumping during transport. Fine if you are keeping it in its shredded state, like tacos or topping chili. But if you are going for a melted state, those anti-coagulation properties actually work against you because they don't melt properly. So, when you go to slice something like pizza or lasagna, the cheese becomes a solid sheet. Bite into it and you'll probably take the entire cheese layer with it. Or in mac & cheese, instead of that creamy texture you crave, your cheese sauce will actually become separated. When you take the time to shred fresh cheeses, you are not only rewarded with amazing flavor, fresh taste, and epic cheese pulls, but also even distribution between bites.

For the perfect meltiness for your nachos, mac & cheese, lasagna, and pizza, you need to grate fresh cheese. A "grate" (hahaha..... sorry) box grater is a cheap purchase and you can use it for grating everything! Grate onions to mix into burger meat. Grate ginger for any recipe! Grate pears and add them into Asian inspired marinades! And most "old school" 4-sided graters have a slicing side, so if you don't have a mandolin slicer, you can use that to evenly slice veggies for soups and salads. Or your food processor may have a grating disk included which will make quick work of that block of cheddar.

Just note, if you grate fresh cheese and store the extras, the strands will start merging together into clumps. So just grate what you need and wrap the rest of the block in parchment or wax paper, then loosely wrap in plastic wrap (this helps keep the cheese from absorbing the flavors of the fridge).

THINKING OUTSIDE THE DOUGH

Dill Pickle Pizza

- **flour for dusting**
- **1 lb. of pizza dough**
- **¾ - 1 Cup Alfredo sauce**
- **2 teaspoons garlic powder**
- **1 teaspoon Italian seasoning**
- **2 teaspoons dried dill**
- **1 ½ Cups fresh shredded or sliced mozzarella**
- **sliced dill pickles**
- **grated parmesan**

Pop that pizza stone on the middle rack of your oven and rock it to 450°F. Flour a pizza peel or the back of a sheet pan. Roll out the dough and transfer to the peel or sheet pan.

Spread the Alfredo sauce over the dough, then sprinkle on the garlic powder, Italian seasoning, and dill. Next, spread on the shredded mozzarella. Top with an even layer of pickles in a circular pattern. And finish with a sprinkle of the parmesan.

Slide the pizza onto the pizza stone and cook till the crust becomes golden, about 14 minutes. NOSH!

Buffalo Chicken Za'

- **½ lb. pizza dough**
- **¼ teaspoon garlic powder**
- **⅓ Cup buffalo sauce (such as ours on pg. 56), plus more for drizzling**
- **1 Cup cooked & shredded chicken**
- **4 oz. ball of fresh mozzarella, shredded, sliced or diced**
- **red onion, thinly sliced**
- **¼ Cup crumbled bleu cheese (if desired)**

Oven to 500°F with a pizza stone on the upper rack. Dust a pizza peel with flour.

Mix garlic powder and hot sauce and pour half of the buffalo sauce over chicken and toss to coat.

Dump about 2/3 of the buffalo sauce over the chicken in a bowl or bag and give it a good toss. Meanwhile, flatten the dough into whatever shape you want, giving it a ½" edge for the crust and to hold in the buffalo sauce and cheeses.

Add the chicken, red onion, and mozzarella to the dough. Sprinkle bleu cheese over pizza, then drizzle remaining sauce over pizza. Bake till crust is golden, about 8-12 minutes. Slice and serve!

- 1 lb. pizza dough
- 2 Tablespoons olive oil
- 8 eggs, cracked and scrambled with 2 Tablespoons water
- 1 ¼ Cups shredded provolone
- 2 Cups shredded cheese (pepper jack and mild cheddar works the best here)
- 1 lb. bacon, cooked crispy and coarsely chopped
- ½ lb. bulk pork breakfast sausage browned
- ½ red pepper finely diced
- ½ onion (white or red), diced

BREAKFAST PIZZA

Oven to 425°F degrees. Skip the pizza stone and instead grease a 10"x15" sheet pan.

Let the dough come to room temperature and press it into the sheet pan evenly. If it's fighting with you, let it sit for 15 minutes and try again. It will succumb to your fingertips. Once worked out, press the dough against the edges to give it a raised area to hold in all the goodness. Bake the crust for 7 minutes.

While the dough is cooking, heat a pan over low heat and grease with butter. Add eggs and slowly cook, scrambling with a spatula. You want to undercook the eggs (slightly runny and barely set) because they will finish cooking in the oven. When dough is done pre-baking, spoon the eggs over the dough.

Add rest of ingredients over eggs. Place back into oven for another 12 minutes. Kick on the broiler during the last 2 minutes to really set everything, but carefully watch it. Broilers can go from awesome to fucked in a matter of seconds. Remove, cut into squares, and serve.

Cinnamon Roll Pizza

TOPPING
- ½ Cup old fashioned oats
- 1 stick butter, softened
- ½ Cup brown sugar
- 3 teaspoons cinnamon

ICING
(FEEL FREE TO DOUBLE THIS. YOU CAN NEVER HAVE TOO MUCH ICING)

- 4 Tablespoons unsalted butter
- 1 Cup powdered sugar
- 3 oz. cream cheese, softened
- 1 teaspoon vanilla extract
- 1 lb. pizza

Oven to 400°F. Skip the stone and line a baking sheet with parchment paper. Roll out the dough to a 12"-14" circle (depending on the sheet pan) and place on parchment paper.

In a bowl, mix the **TOPPING** ingredients together and spread evenly over dough. Slide sheet pan into oven and bake for 13-15 minutes. That dough should be golden! Remove from the hot box and let cool for 10 minutes. While it cools, mix all the *ICING* ingredients in a bowl. Too thin? More powdered sugar. Too thick? Cut it with milk, teaspoon at a time.

Pipe, drizzle, pour, dump, ladle, or splash the icing over the pizza. Slice and serve!

CHICKEN PARM- MAZ- SHIO

The Classic Comfort Food

Stay away from the parmesan in the green plastic container in the "Italian Food" aisle. That shit is only about 50% cheese. Head to the deli counter and get yourself a container of fresh imported parmesan and upgrade your pasta glitter! (Better yet, buy a block of it and grind it yourself with a cheese grater!)

INGREDIENTS

- 4 skinless, boneless chicken breast halves
- 2 large eggs, beaten
- 1-2 Cups flour
- 1 ½ Cups panko bread crumbs, or more as needed
- 1 Cup grated parmesan cheese, divided
- 2 teaspoons oregano

- 2 Tablespoons fresh thyme
- ½ Cup oil for frying, or as needed
- fresh mozzarella, cut into small cubes
- chopped fresh basil
- 6-8 deli sliced provolone cheese slices
- Pasta Sauce (pg.28)
- Pasta Noods (boxed or fresh pg. 102)

DIRECTIONS

Grab that oven dial and rock it to 425°F, place a rack dead center in the oven.

If those chicken breasts are huge, lay them on a cutting board and slice them horizontally. Place chicken between two sheets of plastic or in a freezer bag on a solid, level surface. Start hammering that chicken with the smooth side of a meat mallet till you hit a thickness of about 1/2-inch. There is a good chance these are huge now, so feel free to slice them into smaller portions. Think the size of your palm and fingers laid flat. Sprinkle chicken thoroughly with salt and pepper.

Set up a dredging station. Place the flour into a wide shallow bowl. Beat eggs in another shallow bowl. Mix bread crumbs, ¾ Cup parmesan cheese, oregano, and thyme in a third shallow bowl. Keep the bowls in this order.

Press the chicken breasts into the flour, flip the breasts, and press again then shake off the excess flour. Next, dunk the flour coated chicken in the egg. Remove and let excess egg drip off. Then place the eggy chicken breast into the panko mixture, pressing firmly to pack the breading on, flip, and repeat. Lastly, move to a foil lined sheet pan or baking dish. After the last breast, let rest for 15 minutes.

Heat up ½" olive oil in your largest skillet on medium-high heat. Carefully place the chicken in the hot oil and fry till golden, about 2 minutes per side. Do not crowd the pan! Do it in batches if need be. Oh, and don't freak out if the chicken is not fully cooked. We will finish it in the oven.

Transfer chicken back to the baking dish or sheet pan. Top each breast with 2-3 Tablespoons of tomato sauce, then the mozzarella cheese, remaining ¼ Cup parmesan, basil, and provolone cheese. (If using deli sliced provolone, just rip it apart to blanket the top of the chicken.)

Toss in the oven until cheese is browned and bubbly, about 15 to 20 minutes. Turn the pan half way through cooking to compensate for any hot spots your oven may have.

Serve chicken over cooked pasta noods, and top with more sauce. Or, my personal favorite, between two halves of a warmed crusty Italian or French roll, smothered in extra sauce!

Eggplant Parmesan

Don't Hate

The complaints against Eggplant Parm is usually "too soggy" or "kinda slimy". That's because you can't treat the eggplant the same way as chicken! And skipping the draining step is the first way to ruin this dish.

USE ALL THE SAME INGREDIENTS AS OUR CHICKEN PARM RECIPE, BUT REPLACE THE BUCK-BUCK WITH 2-3 LARGE EGGPLANTS, PEELED AND CUT INTO ¼" ROUNDS.

Before you start cooking, you need to "drain" the eggplant." (I'm sorry. There is no other way to phrase that... damn you internet and emojis!)

2 hours before cooking, peel and slice the eggplant. Lay the slices on a cooling rack over a tray or sink and sprinkle Kosher salt over the eggplant. After an hour, flip the slices and repeat. Don't worry, this will not make the eggplant crazy salty. Occasionally pat the tops dry with paper towel. This is the step most skipped (because it's time consuming) but will result in perfectly textured Eggplant Parmesan.

After 2 or more hours, follow the Chicken Parm Recipe with Eggplant in place of the chicken.

Remember that Zoodle craze a few years ago where people were substituting pasta noods for sprialized zucchini? How many tried it and were left with a plate of basically soup by the end of the meal and the only al dente thing was the cold pizza you ate afterwards cause you couldn't stomach eating those soggy fake wannabe noodles? The culprit? WATER! AGUA! H_2O!

Veggies from the Gourd Family (zucchini, pumpkin, squash, etc.) as well as from the Nightshade Family (eggplant, peppers, etc.) have a surprising amount of liquid hiding inside. When you cook something, anything really, you are reducing the water in the ingredients to concentrate the flavor. If you just dice up the eggplant and toss it in a pan to cook, the heat is going to pull that moisture out. But when making something like stir fry, you don't want that liquid (or as little as possible) coming out during cooking, since stir-fry cooks in about 10 minutes. The same applies to eggplant parm. You carefully dredge and bread the eggplant. When you go to cook it, what happens? The heat from the oven steams the water in the eggplant. The steam has to escape, which leads to soggy breading. And the heat from the oven will not be enough to evaporate the majority of the water.

By salting the eggplant or sprialized zucchini, you are pulling out that excess moisture AND seasoning the veggies from the inside. Less water means firmer texture and bold flavors. Zoodles are actually pretty damn good if made right!

CHICKEN NUGS

Nugs or Fingers... a childhood classic for adults!

Bake 'um or fry 'um up! Either way, get the sauces ready!

FRIED

- **3 lbs. boneless skinless chicken breast**
- **1 Cup dill pickle juice**
- **½ Cup whole milk**
- **2 teaspoons paprika**
- **1 Cup all-purpose flour**
- **1 Cup plain breadcrumbs**
- **3 Tablespoons corn starch**
- **2 Tablespoons garlic powder**
- **1 Tablespoon Kosher salt**
- **1 teaspoon black pepper**
- **3 eggs, well beaten**
- **additional 1-2 Cups of flour (for dredging)**
- **oil, for frying (at least 1" deep)**

DIRECTIONS

Cut the chicken into irregular chunks. Dump the pickle juice, milk, and paprika into a bag and add the chicken. The vinegar in the pickle juice creates a form of "buttermilk"... but with a bit more tang. Give the bag a good shake to coat every piece. Let sit at least an hour in the fridge. Overnight is even better!

Turn on the deep fryer or heat the oil in a large deep pot to 375°F.

In a bowl, whisk the flour, breadcrumbs, corn starch, garlic powder, salt, and pepper. Set aside. Place the additional flour in another bowl. Set up your dredging station as follows: chicken, plain flour, eggs, breadcrumb mixture.

Dump the chicken into a colander to drain. Dip each piece of chicken in the plain flour, then coat in the egg. Next, press into the breadcrumb mixture, coating completely, and then carefully add to the fryer.

Cook in small batches to maintain the oil temperature, keeping it between 350°F-375°F. Fry for 3-5 minutes, depending on the thickness of your chicken. You want a dark golden color with an internal temperature of at least 165°F. Remove to a wire rack to drain slightly before noshing.

Mix the buttermilk, hot sauce, salt, paprika, chili, garlic, and pepper in a zip top bag. Toss in the chicken and refrigerate for 2 hours or overnight.

Heat the oven to 500°F. Spray or brush oil onto a sheet pan (or use silicone mats) and set aside.

Dump the panko into a large, shallow baking dish and toss in the melted butter. Stir the panko till coated, then pop it into the oven. You want to gently toast the panko, so keep a close eye on it. Don't go longer then 4 minutes. Remove from oven and lower temperature to 400°F. Transfer the panko to a large bowl.

Pull the chicken from the marinade and press into the panko. Lay chicken on oiled sheet pan and bake for about 25 minutes, turning once halfway through cooking.

BAKED

- **2 Cups buttermilk (see note below)**
- **1 Tablespoon hot sauce**
- **1 teaspoon Kosher salt**
- **1 teaspoon paprika**
- **1 teaspoon chili powder**
- **1 teaspoon garlic powder**
- **1 teaspoon fresh-ground pepper**
- **2 lbs. boneless, skinless chicken breasts**
- **2 Cups panko breadcrumbs**
- **6 Tablespoons unsalted butter, melted**

No buttermilk? Make it yourself! Just whisk 1 Tablespoon of lemon juice or white vinegar into 1 Cup of whole milk and let sit for 5 minutes.

LEMON CHICKEN ORZO
Light flavors from a single skillet!

Let's keep the dishes to a minimum by cooking in a single skillet. Cast iron or a shallow Dutch oven will work the best here since it will go from stovetop to oven.

INGREDIENTS

- **2 Tablespoons extra virgin olive oil**
- **½ Tablespoon Kosher salt**
- **1 lb. trimmed chicken breasts**
- **2 lemons, sliced into rounds**
- **2 Tablespoons unsalted butter**
- **3 cloves garlic, minced or grated**
- **1 Cup orzo pasta, uncooked (or another tiny pasta. See below.)**
- **⅓ Cup cheap white wine**
- **2 ½ Cups chicken stock**
- **½ bunch of spinach, trimmed of hard stems**
- **zest from one large lemon, then....**
- **all the juice from that one zested lemon**
- **½ Tablespoon dried dill**

DIRECTIONS

Rock the oven to 400°F. Pop an oven safe skillet or Dutch oven on the cooktop over medium high.

Sprinkle the salt over the chicken breasts and give it a quick massage, working the salt into the meat. Add oil to the skillet and heat until it starts to shimmer.

Pop the chicken in and sear for 3-5 minutes, each side. Once seared, move the chicken to a plate.

Now plop the butter in the skillet and once melted, add the lemon slices and cook 1 minute on each side. Make sure the lemon has a nice sear. Remove from skillet and add to the plate with the chicken.

Now add the orzo (or other pasta) to the skillet and cook for 1 minute. Add garlic and stir with the dried pasta for another minute. Slowly dump in the wine, scrapping the bottom of the skillet for those little bits of brown tasty gold (aka: de-glaze the pan).

Next add in the chicken stock, spinach, and lemon juice and bring it to a boil over high heat, stirring occasionally. Place the seared chicken, seared lemons, and any juices from the plate into the skillet.

Transfer skillet to oven and cook uncovered for about 15 minutes. Once chicken is cooked all the way through, remove and serve. Top chicken with lemon zest and dill and nosh away!

THE TINY DEETS ON THE "LITTLE PASTA"

Orzo, or in Italy, risi (which actually means rice), is a very small, rice shaped pasta usually made from semolina. You can treat it like pasta where you cook it in a pot of salted water, then drain... OR... you can treat it like rice and cook it with a 2-1 liquid to orzo ratio. This cooking method will result in a creamier finish since you are basically retaining all the starch from the orzo. Also, cooking it the same way as rice only takes about half the time as rice itself, so it's perfect for those quickie meals. Orzo can be made into a pilaf, or as a substitute for risotto. If adding to soups, add during the last 10 minutes of cooking to ensure it doesn't turn to mush. Orzo alternatives are ditalini, stelline (those tiny shaped stars), or pastaina.

FRieD RiCe
Purposely make leftover rice!

This dish comes together extremely fast, so it's important to have all your ingredients measured and laid out, ready to go. Although you can make this in a pan, a wok is optimal. Its high sides help by pulling the food off the direct heat surface so it doesn't get overcooked.

THE NIGHT BEFORE: *Make 3 Cups of rice. Immediately after cooking, put in container and pop it in the fridge. We have to solidify the starches. Freshly made rice will not work and it will become mush!*

INGREDIENTS

- 2 Tablespoons neutral oil (canola, vegetable, peanut)
- 4 green onions, white and green parts, diced
- 1 medium carrot, peeled and finely diced
- 2 large cloves of garlic, minced
- 2 teaspoons minced ginger (or 1 teaspoon ginger powder)
- 3 Tablespoons soy sauce
- 1 Tablespoon toasted sesame oil
- 3 Cups cooked, chilled rice
- 2 Cups cooked proteins (steak, pork, chicken, shrimp, ham, tofu, etc.)
- ½ Cup frozen peas, defrosted (optional)
- 2 large eggs, lightly beaten with a pinch of Kosher salt

DiRECTiONS

Heat the oil over high heat. Don't freak out if you see it start to smoke. Add in the green onions and carrots. Stir-fry for **2 minutes.** Add the garlic and ginger, stir-fry for **1 minute.** Pour in the soy sauce and sesame oil and allow to heat up for 30 seconds. Carefully dump in the rice and break it up in the pan/wok. Keep everything moving in the pan for **2-3 minutes**. Add your chosen proteins, peas, and egg. Keep stirring until the egg fully cooks, breaking it up as you go, about **2 minutes**. *Serve.*

WANT TO BUY A WOK? THEY ARE AN AMAZING ADDITION TO YOUR KITCHEN, ALLOWING YOU TO FRY, STEAM, AND RAPIDLY COOK. HELL, YOU CAN EVEN MAKE POPCORN IN THEM (JUST MAKE SURE YOU HAVE A LID FOR IT). NOTHING BEATS THE NEWER CARBON STEEL MODELS AVAILABLE. RELATIVELY CHEAP, THEY DO REQUIRE A BIT OF CARE, ALONG THE LINES OF CAST IRON, BUT THEY DISTRIBUTE HEAT EVENLY ACROSS THE WHOLE SURFACE. DON'T WANT TO DEAL WITH THAT?! MODERN NON-STICK VERSIONS ARE GREAT AND EASIER ON THE POCKETBOOK. LOOK FOR A FLAT BOTTOM, 14" WIDE WITH DUAL HANDLES. AND ALWAYS USE BAMBOO OR SILICONE UTENSILS WHEN COOKING WITH IT.

FLAVOR COMBOS!

HAWAIIAN: Use diced Spam and shrimp as your proteins, and add 1 Cup of diced pineapple and 1 Cup diced red pepper (cook red pepper with onions, and pineapple with the proteins). Add a heavy splash of your favorite teriyaki sauce towards the end of cooking.

VEGGIE: Swap the proteins with 1-2 Cups of mushrooms and 1 Cup diced tofu.

LOW CARB: Swap out the rice for frozen riced cauliflower. Add in with onions, as it takes a bit longer to cook up. Make sure most of the moisture is evaporated before adding in oils.

STIR FRY

The ultimate "clean out the fridge" dish!

Simple and easy to make with no end to the customization you can do! Veggies, meats, sauces... the limit is your imagination! Go nuts... or just add them!

INGREDIENTS

- ⅔ **Cup soy sauce**
- 1 **Tablespoon cornstarch**
- 1 **Tablespoon rice wine vinegar**
- ¼ **Cup brown sugar**
- 2 **Tablespoons minced garlic**
- 2 **Tablespoons minced fresh ginger**
- ¼ **teaspoon red pepper flakes**
- 3 **skinless, boneless chicken breast halves, thinly sliced**
- 1 **Tablespoon sesame oil**
- 4 **cups of veggies total (bell peppers, broccoli, water chestnuts, bamboo shoots, snap peas, diced carrots, onion, etc.)**
- 1 **Tablespoon sesame oil**
- 2 **Cups cooked rice**

 *To make this vegetarian, replace the chicken with tofu, mushrooms, or add 2 more cups of veggies.*

Mix soy sauce, corn starch, vinegar, brown sugar, garlic, ginger, and red pepper flakes in a bowl till smooth. Place sliced chicken in a zip top bag and pour the mixture over chicken. Give the bag a good mushing to coat all the chicken pieces. Refrigerate for at least 30 minutes or up to 2 hours.

Cook rice according to directions. While it's cooking, pop a wok or large skillet over high heat and drizzle in the sesame oil. Once hot, toss in your chosen veggies and stir fry for about 3 minutes.

Make a well in the middle of the veggies by pushing them up the wall of the wok or to the outer edges of the skillet. Pour in the final Tablespoon of sesame oil. Remove chicken from the marinade but *DO NOT* discard the marinade. Once the oil is hot, layer in the chicken and cook for about 2 minutes per side. As the chicken cooks, start stirring in the veggies around it. Once the chicken is no longer pink, dump in the reserved marinade and crank the heat to high. Bring the wok/skillet to a boil and cook for another 5-7 minutes, the liquid will thicken and evaporate. Once it hits the perfect "saucy" stage, serve over cooked rice.

"Mise en place" is a French culinary term that means "everything in its place." That means have everything prepped and ready to go for the recipe. Is it detrimental? Not always. But it will make your cooking experience less stressful. And sometimes it actually is critical. Making the Fried Rice on the previous page? That entire dish comes together in about 7 minutes over very, very high heat. If you have to stop to peel and dice carrots in the middle of cooking, you will have a brick of burnt food and a lot of scrubbing on that pan to do.

Asian Chicken Lettuce Wraps

Easy to make, fun to nosh! And kid friendly!

Comes together with simple ingredients. Control the level of heat by adjusting the gochujang sauce. Bib or Boston lettuce works the best, but Romain leaves will work in a pinch. Stay away from iceberg lettuce for this dish. The structure of the leaves is too weak and it offers no flavor.

INGREDIENTS

- 2 Cups mushrooms, diced
- 1 ½ lbs. raw chicken breast, diced small
- 2 Tablespoons vegetable oil
- 3 cloves garlic, chopped
- 1 Tablespoon minced ginger
- Kosher salt and black pepper
- zest of 1 large orange
- 1 small red bell pepper, diced
- 1 can sliced water chestnuts, drained, and chopped into small pieces
- 3 green onions, whites and green parts, chopped
- 3 Tablespoons gochujang or hoisin (available at most supermarkets)
- Bib, Boston, Romaine or similar lettuce leaves (you want undamaged leaves, so be picky in your selection)

DIRECTIONS

Prep the mushrooms by removing tougher parts of the stems and wiping with a damp cloth or soft bristle brush to remove dirt. Do not submerge mushrooms in water. Chop into small pieces and set aside.

Prep the lettuce leaves. Peel the leaves off, being careful not to break or damage them. Gently wash the leaves and pat dry. Set aside.

Pop a skillet or wok over high heat and drizzle oil in. Once hot, add chicken and stir fry for about **2 minutes**. Since the pieces are small it will cook fast. Next, dump in the diced mushrooms and cook another **2 minutes**. Add in ginger, garlic, salt, and pepper, and stir for **another minute** or so to coat everything evenly. Add zest, red bell pepper, water chestnut pieces, and green onions and cook for **another minute**. Pour in gochujang or hoisin and toss all ingredients to coat evenly. Once hot, remove to a serving bowl.

To assemble, pile the BBQ chicken mixture inside the lettuce leaf and nosh. For added flavor, serve with sliced oranges to squeeze over the chicken mixture.

To make this vegetarian, replace chicken with meatless crumbles or pressed and ground tofu.

Always check the International aisles at your supermarket for spices BEFORE the "spice aisle". You can often find better and purer quality for a fraction of the price.

SHEET PAN FAJITAS

The quickest way to make incredible fajitas

Sure, you can make these in a skillet, but for the best and juiciest flavors, a sheet pan is the way to go! Bonus, you get those slightly charred "roasted" flavors from the direct dry heat. Best part, after cooking, just toss the sheet of aluminum foil for the easiest clean up ever!

MAKE IT HAWAIIAN! REPLACE THE OIL WITH COCONUT OIL, USE SHRIMP AS THE PROTEIN, AND ADD IN RINGS OF FRESH PINEAPPLE TO THE VEGGIES! MAKE SURE YOU GET A NICE CHAR ON THOSE RINGS FOR SOME AMAZING FLAVOR!

INGREDIENTS

Proteins:

- 3 Tablespoons vegetable or canola oil
- 3 Tablespoons fresh lime juice
- 1 Tablespoon ground cumin
- 1 Tablespoon chili powder
- 1 ½ teaspoons garlic powder
- 1 ½ teaspoons Kosher salt
- 1 ½ lbs. of whatever protein you desire (chicken breast or flank steak, cut into strips)
- splash of tequila (optional)

Veggies:

- 2 Tablespoons vegetable or canola oil
- 2 Tablespoons lime juice
- 1 sweet onion, halved and sliced
- 2 bell peppers, seeded and cut into strips
- 1 small jalapeño pepper, seeded and chopped
- pinch of salt

DIRECTIONS

Kick the oven up to 425°F. In a zip top bag, mix the oil, cumin, chili powder, garlic powder, salt, and tequila (if using). Once mixed, toss in your protein of choice. Give it a good squish to coat the proteins, and let marinate in the fridge for at least an hour or overnight.

In a large bowl, toss all the ingredients for the veggies together, making sure everything is coated nicely.

Dump the bag of protein into a strainer and give it a good toss to remove excess marinade. Dump the strainer onto a foil lined sheet pan, making sure all the meat is single layer (touching is okay, overlap is not). Add veggies to sheet pan next to proteins (slight overlap is ok for the veggies). Roast for 10 minutes, rotating pan halfway through. Remove from oven and kick on the broiler. Return pan to under broiler and cook until the veggies start to char and proteins are fully cooked, 3-5 minutes.

Serve with tortillas and your favorite fajita sides, or serve over rice for a fajita bowl!

IF THE THOUGHT OF ROASTING RAW VEGGIES NEXT TO RAW PROTEINS GIVES YOU THE WILLIES, JUST USE 2 SMALLER SHEET PANS, ONE FOR THE VEGGIES, ONE FOR THE MEATS. BUT TRUST ME, YOU ARE COOKING THIS IN A TEMPERATURE OVER 3X'S THE SURVIVABLE LIMIT FOR THE ICKIES. NOTHING THAT CAN HURT YOU IS GOING TO SURVIVE.

To make this vegetarian, replace chicken with sliced strips of extra firm tofu. Just be gentle when "mushing it around" as you marinate it so you don't destroy the tofu. Also, depending on how thick you slice the tofu, you may need to roast it in the oven for 30 minutes prior to roasting the veggies. So roast the tofu, then add the veggies to the tray for the last 10 min.

GO BOWLS DEEP!

Endless Customization

The limits here are literally what is available in your pantry. These are great to make and experiment with to really get a grasp on how flavors come together. Here's some starter recipes to get you going.

Chicken Fajita Bowl
Makes 2 Big Ass Bowls

- 2 limes, zested and juiced
- 3 Tablespoons fajita seasoning
- 1 heaping Tablespoon diced chipotles in adobo
- Kosher salt
- 2 large skinless, boneless chicken breasts
- 1 Tablespoon vegetable oil
- 1 large red pepper, sliced into strips
- 1 large orange pepper, sliced into strips
- ½ large yellow onion, thick sliced
- ¼ Cup cilantro, roughly chopped
- 1 can black beans, drained but not rinsed
- 2 large avocados
- 2-3 Cups cooked basmati or jasmine rice
- 1 Cup broken tortilla strips
- Baja or Avocado Sauce (pg. 22)

Oven to 375°F. Sprinkle salt onto chicken breasts, then rub the chipotle peppers and adobo sauce onto the breasts. The more chipotle peppers, the hotter the spice level. Then sprinkle with fajita seasoning. Place on sheet pan.

Toss peppers and onions with zest, lime juice, cilantro, and oil. Dump onto sheet pan with chicken and bake for 18-20 minutes, until chicken reads 165°F. Keep an eye on the veggies. They may need less or more time depending how thick they were cut.

While chicken and veggies bake, heat black beans in small pot. Slice and pit avocados. Remove chicken and let rest for 5 minutes, then slice into 1" strips. Scoop rice into bowl, then top 1/3 of bowl with sliced chicken, 1/3 with veggies, and 1/3 with black beans and avocado. Top with tortilla strips and sauce.

Sushi Bowl
Makes 2 Big Ass Bowls

- 3 Cups cooked short grain or sushi rice
- 3 Tablespoons seasoned rice vinegar
- 8 oz. raw shrimp, peeled and deveined
- 1 avocado, thinly sliced
- 1 English cucumber, quartered and sliced
- Kosher salt
- 3 Tablespoons seasoned rice vinegar
- 1 large carrot, peeled and sliced thin
- 4 Tablespoons mayonnaise
- 1-2 Tablespoons sriracha
- 2 Tablespoons lemon juice
- pickled ginger
- diced tuna or salmon (optional, make sure it is sashimi grade from a reputable store)
- 1 shredded nori sheet (optional)
- toasted sesame seeds (optional)

Start by quartering the cucumber lengthwise, then slice. Sprinkle slices with a bit of salt then toss in seasoned rice vinegar. Set aside.

Next, cook the shrimp. Flavor is all up to you, but our go to is either a splash of teriyaki sauce, or toss shrimp in a sweet chili sauce, then cook in a bit of sesame oil.

While shrimp is cooking, whisk the mayo, sriracha, and lemon juice till smooth. Set aside.

Stir 2 Tablespoons seasoned rice vinegar into the rice till incorporated, then scoop rice into bowls. Top half the bowl with shrimp. Next, add a line of cucumber, a line of carrots, a line of sliced avocado, and finish with a bit of pickled ginger off to the side of the bowl. Drizzle mayo/sriracha mix over entire bowl then top with shredded nori and sesame seeds if preferred.

GO BOWLS DEEP!

Greek Chicken Bowl
Makes 2 Big Ass Bowls

A pressure cooker makes this one super easy!

- 2 lbs. boneless, skinless chicken breasts
- Kosher salt and pepper
- ¼ Cup olive oil
- 1 teaspoon dried oregano
- 2 teaspoons paprika
- 2 teaspoons minced garlic (about 4 cloves)
- 1 Cup couscous
- 1 Cup plain Greek yogurt
- 2 Tablespoons lemon juice
- 4 oz. crumbled feta
- 1 English cucumber, quartered and chopped
- 1 pint cherry tomatoes, quartered
- 1 Cup kalamata olives, pitted & chopped
- 3 Tablespoons fresh dill, chopped (divided)

Sprinkle salt and pepper onto the chicken. In the cooker, mix together the spices, 1 teaspoon minced garlic, oil, and ½ Cup water. Lay the chicken in the mixture, spooning some onto the tops of the breasts. Lock the top and pressure cook on high, 6 minutes. Once the cycle is complete, quick release the pot and remove the chicken to a cutting board to rest.

Dump the couscous into the hot liquid, sprinkle with salt and pepper, give a quick stir to combine, and cover the cooker with a lid to trap in the heat and moisture and let sit for about 7-8 minutes until tender. Before the couscous is done, slice, chop, or dice the chicken to your liking.

Now mix together the yogurt, lemon juice, 1 teaspoon minced garlic, and 1 Tablespoon fresh dill. Spread ½ Cup of the yogurt sauce on the bottom of a bowl. Top with couscous, cucumbers, tomatoes, olives, sliced chicken, and feta. Finish with a sprinkle of the fresh dill.

(Feel free to double the yogurt mixture to drizzle some onto the bowls or to dip some naan into.)

A bowl is only limited by what you have in your kitchen. These are great because they allow you to really play with flavors. A "perfect" bowl is one that has contrasting elements to it, and that can be anything from texture (soft and crunchy), flavor (sweet vs. savory), or spice levels (spicy vs. cool). Even temperatures (hot rice vs. cold flavored shrimp)! So here is a very basic how-to in building a bowl:

BASE: 1-2 Cups of starch. rice, brown rice, couscous, sushi rice, lentils, pasta, ripped up tortilla shells. This will fill the bottom of your bowl, no more than half the height of your chosen bowl.

PROTEIN: Steak, chicken, tofu, shrimp, fish, buffalo, dinosaur, unicorn... whatever you choose, this will be the main flavor. The protein will take up about 1/3 of the top of your bowl.

SIDE CAR: These are your main flavor pairings. Doing fajita chicken? This is your grilled onions and peppers. Shrimp bowl? This might be your marinated cucumbers and avocado slices. Steak bowl? Try roasted potatoes or corn. The side car takes up the middle 1/3 of the bowl.

ADD ONS: This is anything you want to enhance flavor or texture. This could be black beans, raw onions, guac, pickled ginger, matchstick carrots, salsa... anything to bring the harmony of the bowl together.

TOPPINGS: Sprinkle of cheese, drizzle of a spicy wasabi, splash of sriracha, sesame seeds, or tortilla strips... this ties the entire bowl's flavor and texture together.

Cook starchy foods (like rice, lentils, pasta, etc.) in stock rather than water to add a whole new layer of flavor.

JAMBALAYA

The heart of NOLA, the flavors of heaven

Make this your own by swapping out the protein (or using a variety). A hearty dish that fills you up. Control the heat by adjusting the red pepper freely. Scales nicely, and has a certain amount of freedom to adjust the amount of veggies without sacrificing quality.

INGREDIENTS

- 3 Tablespoons olive oil, divided
- 1 large white onion, diced
- 2 medium red bell peppers, cored and diced
- 3 ribs celery, diced
- 1 jalapeño pepper, seeded and finely chopped
- 2 boneless skinless chicken breasts, diced
- 5 cloves garlic, peeled and smashed
- 15 oz. can of crushed tomatoes
- 4 Cups chicken stock
- 1 ½ Cups uncooked long grain white rice (DO NOT USE QUICK COOK RICE!)
- 3 Tablespoons Cajun seasoning
- 1 teaspoon dried thyme
- ¼ teaspoon red pepper
- 1 lb. andouille sausage, halved lengthwise then sliced into thin half rings
- 1 large bay leaf
- 1 lb. raw large shrimp, peeled/deveined
- 1 Cup thinly-sliced okra OR 1 Tablespoon filé powder (or both... fuck it!)
- Kosher salt and freshly-cracked black pepper

DIRECTIONS

Heat 2 Tablespoons of the oil in a stock pot over medium-high heat. Add the diced onion and sauté for 2 minutes, stirring occasionally. Then dump in the peppers, celery, and jalapeño. Sauté for an additional 5 minutes. Make a well in the middle of the sautéing veggies and add the remaining Tablespoon of oil. Next, dump in the diced chicken. Stir occasionally until chicken is cooked through. Pop in the crushed garlic and sauté for an additional 30 seconds.

Ramp the heat up to high. Dump in the crushed tomatoes, stock, rice, Cajun seasoning, thyme, red pepper, bay leaf, and andouille. Give it a good stir. Bring to a bubbling simmer then lower heat to a medium-low, cover the pot and cook for 30 minutes, stirring every 5 minutes or so to keep rice from burning to the bottom of the pot.

Taste test the rice. It should be just about done, but still have an "al dente" feel to it.

Add the shrimp, okra, and give it another good stir. Cook till shrimp is no longer gray, about 3-5 minutes. Add in filé powder (if using, SEE NOTES). Taste your masterpiece and adjust seasonings. Like it hotter, add more red pepper. Need more "Cajun" kick, add more of that seasoning. Start with 2 teaspoons of salt and 1 teaspoon of pepper and adjust from there. Serve and nosh away!

NOTES: OKRA AND FILÉ POWDER HAVE NATURAL THICKENING PROPERTIES. IF USING BOTH IN YOUR DISH, YOU MAY HAVE TO ADD ½-1 CUP MORE OF STOCK. YOU DON'T WANT AN OVERALL THICKNESS LIKE CHILI BUT YOU ALSO DON'T WANT A SOUP-LIKE CONSISTENCY.
(SEE NEXT PAGE FOR WHAT FILÉ POWDER IS.)

LOADED GUMBO

Laissez les bons temps rouler, bitches!

I'm sure the addition of tomatoes to my gumbo is going to seriously piss off a few true Creoles. But I'm employing an elevated version of the Spanish Soffrito, which uses onion, garlic, bell peppers, and tomatoes for a rich umami base.

- ½ **Cup Flour**
- ½ **Cup vegetable or canola oil**
- **2 lbs. medium raw shrimp, defrosted and peeled**
- **3 large stalks celery, diced**
- **2 large bell peppers, cored and diced**
- **2 Tablespoons minced garlic (about 6-8 large cloves)**
- **1 Cup peeled, seeded, and diced tomato (or 1 can of diced tomato, minus juices)**
- ½ **teaspoon red pepper (or more)**
- **1 teaspoon black pepper**
- **1 Tablespoon Kosher salt**
- **1 teaspoon dried thyme**
- **3 bay leaves**
- **4 Cups chicken stock**
- **1 lb. andouille sausage, sliced into half moons**
- **1-2 Tablespoon(s) filé powder**
- **okra (optional)**
- **cooked rice for serving**

COOKING WARNING!!!

MAKING THE ROUX HERE WILL SERIOUSLY BURN IF YOU ACCIDENTALLY SPLASH IT ONTO YOUR SKIN. IT'S THICK AND WILL STICK! WHEN STIRRING, USE A METAL OR SILICONE WHISK AND SLOWLY STIR THE MIXTURE.

THE SCAR ON MY LEFT WRIST WILL TESTIFY TO THIS FACT!

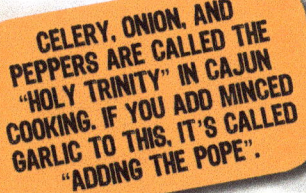

CELERY, ONION, AND PEPPERS ARE CALLED THE "HOLY TRINITY" IN CAJUN COOKING. IF YOU ADD MINCED GARLIC TO THIS, IT'S CALLED "ADDING THE POPE".

Get the oven roaring to 350°F. In a Dutch oven, pour the oil and sprinkle in the flour. Whisk till combined and place in the preheated oven for a minimum of 2 hours, stirring every 30 minutes *(SEE WARNING ABOVE)*. You can let it go longer then 2 hours to achieve a deeper, "nuttier" flavor from the flour, but only take it to a dark brown color.

While the roux is in the oven, defrost the frozen raw shrimp in a cold-water bath, refreshing the water every 15 minutes. Once fully defrosted, peel and devein the shrimp. Place prepared shrimp in the fridge till ready to use.

Once the roux is done, remove from the oven and pop it over medium-high heat. Slowly add the onions, celery, and green peppers and cook, stirring constantly for 7 minutes. Toss in the garlic and cook for another minute. Add in the diced tomatoes, seasonings, okra (if using), and bay leaves. Stir to combine and pour in stock while stirring. Turn heat to low, dump in the sausage, place lid on, and cook for 60 minutes. Add in the shrimp and cook another 5 minutes until the shrimp is no longer gray. Add the filé powder, stir, and cover for 10 minutes. The gumbo should thicken quite a bit. If not, add a bit more filé powder. Serve over rice.

WTF is filé powder?

FILÉ POWDER IS THE GROUND YOUNG LEAVES OF THE SASSAFRAS TREE THAT ADDS A DISTINCTIVE, EARTHY FLAVOR AND TEXTURE. WHEN NOT USING OKRA, FILÉ POWDER CAN SERVE AS A THICKENING AGENT. OFTEN THIS IS NOT STIRRED IN UNTIL THE LAST MINUTE OF COOKING. IF YOUR LOCAL STORE DOESN'T CARRY IT, YOU CAN SEARCH ONLINE. BUY A SMALL CONTAINER. A LITTLE GOES A LONG WAY.

PASTA-IAYA

Cajun + Italian = a delicious mash-up!

Swapping the rice for noodles and incorporating some Italian seasonings, this pan made dish comes together in a single pot for a quick and satisfying weeknight meal!

INGREDIENTS

- 1 Tablespoon olive oil
- 1 lb. andouille sausage, sliced into ¼" rounds
- 1 lb. boneless, skinless chicken breast or thighs, diced into 1" chunks
- 1 bell pepper, cored and diced
- 4 stalks of celery, finely diced
- 1 onion, finely diced
- 4 cloves minced garlic
- 1 Tablespoon paprika
- 1 teaspoon dried basil
- 1 teaspoon dried thyme leaves
- 1 teaspoon dried oregano
- 1 (28 oz.) can crushed tomatoes
- 1 ½ Cups chicken stock
- 1 lb. pasta (penne or fettuccini)
- 1 lb. peeled and deveined shrimp
- salt to taste

When a recipe calls for sautéing onions and garlic, DO NOT ADD THEM IN AT THE SAME TIME! Onions take about 8 minutes to cook down. Garlic takes 30 seconds. Onions get better the longer they cook. Garlic gets bitter and can ruin a dish.

DIRECTIONS

Grab your largest skillet with a lid and pop that over medium heat. Drizzle in the olive oil and toss in the andouille. Once the sausage starts cooking and releasing some of its fats, turn up the heat to medium high and start cooking that chicken. Cook while stirring until the chicken starts to brown.

Now toss in all the veggies and spices and cook until the veggies start to soften. Dump in the crushed tomatoes, juices and all, and simmer for 10-12 minutes.

Add the chicken stock, rip the heat to high and get it all boiling. Stir the dried pasta directly into the pan.

Cook for about 8 minutes, or until the pasta is al dente. Toss in the shrimp and continue to cook for another 5 minutes, stirring every minute or so. If the dish is getting a bit on the "thick" side, just drizzle in more stock to loosen it up a bit. Serve!

Pressure Cooker Chicken Lollypops

A savory meal that is incredibly customizable!

If you happen to have one of those new-fangled electric pressure cookers that were all the rage a few years ago, you can take advantage of the cheap price of chicken drummies.

BASE INGREDIENTS

2 lbs. chicken drumsticks, skin removed or kept on, dealer's choice.

MONGOLIAN

- ¾ Cup chicken broth
- ½ Cup low sodium soy sauce
- 1 Tablespoon rice wine vinegar
- 1 Tablespoon sesame oil
- ½ Cup brown sugar
- 4 cloves garlic minced
- 1 ½ Tablespoon ginger

GARNISH: sesame seeds

GARLIC GINGER

- ½ Cup chicken broth
- ½ Cup soy sauce
- 2 Tablespoons brown sugar
- 3 Tablespoons honey
- 2 Tablespoons rice wine vinegar
- 5 garlic cloves, minced
- 1 Tablespoon ginger
- ½ yellow onion, finely chopped

HONEY LIME

- 1 Cup soy sauce
- ⅓ Cup fresh lime juice
- 4 Tablespoons honey
- 2 Tablespoons green onion
- 2 teaspoons chili powder
- 1 Tablespoon minced garlic
- 2 Tablespoons olive oil

CILANTRO LIME

- 4 cloves minced garlic
- ¾ Cup chicken broth or stock
- 1 Tablespoon cumin
- 1 teaspoon cayenne (red) pepper
- ⅓ Cup lime juice
- 3 Tablespoons chopped cilantro

DIRECTIONS

In a zip top bag, mix all ingredients under the flavor you desire, and shake till all ingredients are mixed (or in the case of sugars, until those are dissolved). Add the chicken drummies. Toss into the fridge to marinate for 2-6 hours, or for the best flavor, overnight.

When ready to cook, remove the drummies from the marinade and stand up on a trivet in your pressure cooker. Pour the marinade into the pot, lock the lid, seal the valve, and pressure cook on high pressure for 15 minutes. Once done, first let a natural release of pressure happen for 15 minutes. Then release all pressure manually (don't burn yourself with the steam). While the chicken is cooking, kick on that oven broiler. Remove chicken and place on foil lined sheet pan/baking dish and brush with liquid from pressure cooker. Place under broiler, 3 minutes per side ,or until they are as done as you would like them to be.

While chicken is broiling, mix 2 Tablespoons cold water with 2 Tablespoons cornstarch. Set pressure cooker to sauté setting. Once sauce is boiling, whisk in cornstarch mix and simmer till thickened, 3-4 minutes. Remove chicken from oven and brush with thickened sauce. Garnish and serve.

GRANDPA'S RIBS

Honoring the man who made me the man AND Chef I am today!

Whether you go with my Grandpa's pressure cooker (he used the old style, lock the lid and pray it doesn't blow up the house kind... but the current electric styles work just as good) method or my slow roasting technique, the end result will be incredibly delicate, fall off the bone, flavor packed, carnivore awesomeness! We will save the advanced smoking method for a later book.

PRESSURE COOKER

- 1 meaty rack of baby back ribs or spare ribs, about 2-3 lbs.
- dry rub of your choosing
- 1 Cup beef broth
- ¼ Cup apple cider vinegar
- liquid smoke
- BBQ sauce

DIRECTIONS

Rinse the ribs under water then pat dry. Massage them with the dry rub, both tops and bottoms.

Place a rack or trivet in the bottom of the pressure cooker. Dump in the broth, apple cider vinegar, and a hearty splash of the liquid smoke (about a Tablespoon or so). Stand the ribs upwards in the pressure cooker (you may have to cut them). Cover and lock the pressure cooker.

Baby Back: 25 Min. High Pressure (or 15 PSI)

Spare Ribs: 35 Min. High Pressure (or 15 PSI)

Naturally release pressure for 15-20 minutes. While cooker is releasing pressure, set a rack in the upper third of your oven and kick on the broiler. Cover a baking sheet with foil. Remove ribs and place on baking sheet. Paint those babies with your favorite BBQ sauce.

Place ribs under broiler for about 2 minutes. Keep a close eye on them, they may burn quick due to the sugars in the sauce. Remove and nosh!

SLOW ROAST

- 2 racks of ribs
- dry rub
- 1 Cup cheap white wine
- ¼ Cup apple cider vinegar
- 2 Tablespoons honey
- 1 Tablespoon liquid smoke
- 3 Tablespoons Worcestershire sauce
- 4 cloves garlic, chopped

DIRECTIONS

Rinse and pat dry the ribs. Rip out two sheets of aluminum foil (heavy duty is preferred here, 2 sheets for each rack of ribs). Place each slab on the foil on a baking tray. Massage the dry rub into the meaty parts of the ribs. Then, working lengthwise, curl the foil up and around each slab of ribs, sealing at the top (think foil packet). Crimp the top sheets by folding over the edges a few times. Then seal only one end of the foil packet the same way. Toss into the fridge for a minimum of 1 hour or max 6 hours.

Rock that oven to a gentle 250°F. On the stovetop in a pot, make the braising liquid by mixing the wine, vinegar, honey, smoke, Worcestershire, and garlic over low heat, and bring to a gentle simmer.

Remove ribs from fridge and pour the braise into the open end of each of the packets. Curl and crimp that end closed. Pop in the oven and braise those babies for about for 2 1/2 hours.

Remove the ribs from the oven. From here, it's your choice. Nosh as they are, or if you choose to slather them with a sauce, rock the broiler and pop them in the oven for about 2 minutes.

LET YOUR MEAT REST! Steaks and chicken, 10-20 minutes. A good-sized turkey you can let rest for an hour (bet that just opened your eyes to timing on Thanksgiving). If your worried about it getting cold, just tent it with foil. Plus, room temp. turkey tastes WAYYYY better then hot.

COQ AU VIN

Bringing the French countryside home

The French translation for this is "Cock with Wine"... and although we've all been there before, this rustic French dish dates back centuries and is the essence of savory! So, grab a bottle of red for the dish, and a bottle of whatever you like for yourself, and let's give drunk cooking a try!

INGREDIENTS

- 4 oz. pancetta, chopped
- 2 Tablespoons olive oil
- salt and pepper to taste
- 1 large yellow onion, diced
- 4 cloves garlic minced or grated
- 2 medium carrots, chopped
- 2 Tablespoons tomato paste
- 3 lbs. boneless chicken thighs, trimmed of excess fat

- 2 Tablespoons flour
- 2 Cups red wine
- 2 Cups chicken broth
- 2 leaves bay
- 6 whole sprigs fresh thyme
- 1 Tablespoon butter
- 2 Cups mushrooms (white or brown, quartered
- ½ Cup fresh parsley chopped

DIRECTIONS

Rock the oven to 275°F.

Grab your large Dutch oven or oven safe pot and pop it on top of the stove over medium heat. Cook the pancetta for 8 minutes until lightly brown. Remove the pancetta to a plate lined with paper towel by using a slotted spoon, leaving the remaining fat behind.

Pat the chicken dry and sprinkle with salt and pepper. In batches, cook the chicken in the pancetta fat till brown, 5 minutes a side. Add olive oil if needed. Move the chicken to the plate with the pancetta.

Add onions and carrots to the pot and cook for 10 to 12 minutes over medium heat, stirring occasionally, and scraping the bottom of the pot, until the onions are lightly browned. Add the garlic and cook for 1 more minute. Dump in the tomato paste and give everything a good stir. Cook for 1 minute. Add pancetta and chicken back into the pot, dump in the wine, chicken broth, bay leaves, and thyme and bring to a simmer. Cover the pot with a lid and place it in the oven for 45-60 minutes.

Remove from the oven and place on top of the stove over medium heat. Mix the butter and flour together first, then add to the stew, stirring until dissolved.

In a medium sauté pan, add olive oil and cook the mushrooms over medium-low heat for 5 to 10 minutes until browned. Dump mushrooms into stew and simmer for another 10 minutes. Nosh.

ALTHOUGH THIS DISH USES A DEEP RED WINE AS A BASE, OTHER VARIATIONS USING AN ARRAY OF WINES DO EXIST, INCLUDING RIESLING, WHITE WINES, AND EVEN CHAMPAGNE. IF YOU REPLACE THE CHICKEN WITH BEEF, THIS DISH BECOMES BEEF BOURGUIGNON. I GUESS "DU BOEUF AU VIN" DOESN'T SOUND AS FANCY.

MR. J's FRESH Pasta Noods

Our own Noodle Guru shares his favorite pasta recipe!

Mr. J knows noods! And although he knows it's a bit of work, the end result will be totally worth it! A pasta roller, either a mixer attachment or free-standing hand cranked one, will save you a ton of time.

INGREDIENTS

- **2 Cups flour, or for best results, "00" flour**
- **3 large eggs**
- **1 Tablespoon olive oil**
- **1 ½ teaspoons Kosher salt**

Mixer Directions

Dump all ingredients into the bowl of your stand mixer with the dough hook attached and mix until a shaggy dough forms. Knead for about 10 more minutes on low until a smooth ball forms.

Remove dough from mixing bowl, form into a ball, and wrap tightly with plastic wrap. Let sit for at least 30 minutes.

By Hand Directions

On a clean work surface shape 1 ½ Cups of flour in a mound. Make a well in the center of the flour and crack eggs into the well, then drizzle in the oil and sprinkle in the salt.

Gently whisk eggs and oil together with a fork or small whisk while slowly incorporating flour from the mound. Once everything is combined, add more flour little by little until dough is no longer sticky. Dough feel too dry? Add 1 teaspoon of water at a time. Knead dough for 8-10 minutes by pressing the heel of your palm into the dough ball, then folding it over and repeating. Wrap tightly with plastic wrap. Let sit for at least 30 minutes.

Follow your pasta machine instructions for rolling out the dough and cutting it into desired pasta type. Or you can roll the dough out by hand with a rolling pin until thin (think the thickness of a penny), then cut into desired shapes/lengths. Lasagna sheets, easy peasy. Spaghetti or linguini will be a test of patience. Use a pizza cutter and a clean ruler for the best chance of clean straight cuts.

DRYING

Lay the cut pasta dough onto a pasta drying rack, the back of your kitchen chairs, off clean hangers, clothesline, or laid out on sheet pans in a single layer (touching ok... overlapping no) and allow pasta to air dry for 24 hours. Remove pasta and store in an airtight container until ready to use. Your pasta should last for up to a month if kept in a cool dry place.

SPINACH: ½ Cup thawed frozen spinach, minced and squeezed dry, blended into the eggs and oil.

SAFFRON: 5 threads saffron soaked in 2 Tablespoons warm water for about 30 minutes. Strain out solids and mix water into dough.

HERBED: 2 Cups of whatever herbs you desire, without the stems. Blend in a food processor with the eggs, oil, and salt. Dump into well of flour and mix together.

SALT THAT PASTA WATER! A teaspoon of salt won't do shit for a pound of pasta. The water should taste like seawater. And don't worry, your noods won't come out tasting like a salt lick. But they will come out being the best tasting noodles you've ever had. Easy ratio is: 1 lb. noodles / 1 gal. water / 2 heaping Tablespoons of Kosher salt.

DEEP FRIED

"You could deep fry a garden hose and someone will dunk it in ranch and eat it."

- Robert Devaroux

"Fried Food tastes great, and people don't seem to mind the fat aspect."

- Eric Schlosser

"Nothing makes me happy quite like a boatload of freshly fried fast food smothered in good ol' MSG."

- Becca Fitzpatrick

THE NITTY GRITTY OF EXTRA CRISPY

Well here we are again... first MSG and now Deep Frying. Show of hands, how many think deep frying is the ultimate evil in life? I've actually heard people say smoking is safer then deep fried foods, and if you know someone like that, get them out of your life. You don't need that type of bullshit clouding your mind.

Are deep fried foods bad for you? Yeah, in the same way that salt, sugar, cupcakes, alcohol, and soda are: In mass and constant quantities. Have 2 doughnuts for breakfast, fries for lunch, and bucket of fried chicken for dinner every day and yeah, shit will start going south in the way of your health. But rocking a batch of fried chicken or fries once a week, balanced out with a somewhat decent diet and moderate exercise isn't going to put you in the ground any faster. If done right, a batch of fries may contain a teaspoon or two of absorbed oil in total. There's more in a standard candy bar.

But here's the problem... most people and businesses do not deep fry properly. Deep frying is almost a science in and of itself. Ever have a killer basket of fries where the outside is crispy and the inside is fluffy white soft, and you barely had to wipe your hands eating them? Those were done right. From starches to water content to batter/breading makeup, there's so much to take into account.

Deep frying occurs when food is lowered into oils heated to 350-375°F. The moisture in the food rapidly heats up, producing steam, and escapes out through the food. In the case of wet batters, the water completely evaporates, leaving the crispy shell. Surface area plays a large part in it. A large shrimp will fry up in 2-3 minutes, a chicken breast in 6-8 minutes.

Now here is where it all goes wrong and why it gets a bad rap: not using proper oils with high smoke points, proper (and right sized) equipment, food prep, etc. You can't just cut up a potato and drop it in hot oil. You need to soak those for a while in cold water to draw out the excess starch. Starch will block the steam from escaping, resulting in a soggy, oily fry. Oil cannot penetrate the food if water is steaming up and escaping... but leave the food in long enough and the moisture disappears, allowing oil to get into the food, making it extra greasy. Fry at a low enough temperature, and you have to leave the food in longer, thus making it really greasy. Jam too much food in the oil and you'll lower the temperature rapidly, probably by 100°F... resulting in a longer frying time and possibly stuck together food, and again, greasy.

BTW: as great as your air fryer is, nothing will quite deliver on an epic crunch like deep frying.

The Secret Ingredient to Deep Frying...

VODKA! By adding it to a wet batter (the kind you dunk the food in), the vodka will help produce a crispier, crunchier crust. Why? Alcohol evaporates the fastest in hot oil, which dries out the batter faster and more violently, resulting in more bubbles, which in turn means more surface area... thus a crispier crust.

Here is a great wet batter recipe we use quite often:

Equal parts by volume of ice cold water, vodka, flour, and cornstarch, with a heavy pinch of salt and baking powder. And whatever you use to measure (measuring cup, Yatzee shaker, empty skull of your enemies, etc), measure the dry first, then the wet. Then whisk together until incorporated.

ARANCINI

Sicily: Rocking fried cheese since the 10th century!

Crispy breading surrounding soft rice surrounding red sauce surrounding mozzarella???
Why are we still talking?!?!? MAKE! NOW!

INGREDIENTS

- 3 Tablespoons extra virgin olive oil
- ½ Cup white wine
- 3 ¾ Cups good chicken stock
- salt
- 1 egg
- 2 Cups arborio (preferred), carnaroli, or even in a pinch, sushi rice
- pasta sauce (jarred or our sauce from pg. 28)
- 4 oz. mozzarella pearls or fresh mozzarella cut into ½" cubes

FOR THE BREADING:

- 1 ½ - 2 Cups flour
- 2 eggs, whisked with 2 Tablespoons vodka
- breadcrumbs

DIRECTIONS

HOURS/DAY BEFORE: Heat the olive oil in a pan over medium high heat and add the rice, sautéing for about 2 minutes. Carefully pour in the wine and stir till mostly absorbed. Now start pouring in the stock, a little at a time, and continuously stir until each bit is absorbed. A ladle is very helpful here. It may seem like a lot of stock, but just keep at it. The rice will eventually suck it all up. After the last of the stock is added, the rice should be done and slightly al dente. Taste the rice, and salt to taste. If the rice is still very firm, add in a bit more stock, but it shouldn't be at this point. Remove from heat, crack the egg into the rice mixture, stir till fully combined, then set in the fridge to cool for a few hours, but overnight is the best.

Once you are ready to make the arancini, remove rice from fridge. In a cupped hand, place some of the chilled rice, forming into a cup shape. Do not place the rice too thin, you need a bit of thickness or the filling will ooze out during cooking. Place a piece or two of mozzarella and a bit of the sauce in the center of the cupped rice. Close your hand around the ball of rice, sealing it into a ball shape with the cheese and sauce sealed in the middle. Set aside on parchment while you build the rest of the balls.

Next, roll the balled rice in flour, then in the beaten eggs, lastly in the breadcrumbs. Repeat with the other rice balls. Set in fridge for 30 minutes to firm up.

Heat canola or vegetable oil in a deep fryer or Dutch oven to 375°F. Carefully add the balls to the hot oil. They will cook quickly, so be sure to watch them and turn if necessary if frying in a shallow pot. Fry for 2 minutes, then remove to paper towel to drain off excess oil. Serve plain, or with a small spoonful of sauce on the plate with the arancini placed on top. Garnish with basil.

Always keep a cheap bottle of red and white wine in your kitchen. And I mean cheap. Cooking with fine wine is a waste of good wine, because in the end, the subtle hints of the good wine are long gone. Peek into any professional kitchen, and chances are you will find either generic boxed wine or that glass gallon jug you can pick up for like 10 bucks.

Mac & Cheese Bites

Your next pot luck just got cheesy!

Got leftovers of our Mac & Cheese from pg. 80??? A quick battering and deep frying will give you the most epic finger food that is a perfect party food!

INGREDIENTS

- **2 lbs. left over mac and cheese, or fresh made and refrigerated for at least 6 hours.**
- **2 Cups flour**
- **2 eggs whisked with 2 Tablespoons vodka**
- **4 Cups regular or panko breadcrumbs**
- **vegetable or canola oil, for deep frying**

DIRECTIONS

Make sure that leftover mac and cheese is chilled... it'll just make it easier to work with. This will go smoother if you set up a "dredging station". Place the flour in one container, the whisked eggs in a second container, and the breadcrumbs in a third, lined up in that order. At the end, place a sheet pan.

Also, don't worry about the vodka. It'll evaporate completely once it hits the oil, so these are safe for the lil' ones to nosh. If it still freaks you out, swap the vodka for cold water or chilled seltzer water.

NOTE: *This is a great time to alter the flavors if you desire. If you made a plain Mac & Cheese, you can add flavors to various parts of the dredging station. Sprinkle Cajun seasoning or chili powder into the flour. Add a few splashes of your favorite hot sauce to the egg wash. Add grated parmesan to the bread crumbs. The only rule to this is do not add any seasonings that contain paprika or any sugars to the breadcrumbs. Paprika has a natural sugar content that will burn very fast when deep fried (adding it to the flour is fine). Sugars just melt in hot oil and will leave you with a mess to clean later.*

You can either cut or roll the Mac & Cheese. Cutting it is quick, but a bit harder to dredge. Rolling it is messier, but a breeze to dredge. Either way, you are aiming for about golf ball sized firm balls (hahahah) of Mac & Cheese.

After you form the Mac & Cheese, roll it in flour, shake off excess, dunk in egg to coat, then roll in breadcrumbs. Shake off excess crumbs and place on sheet tray. Repeat till you have the desired amount of rolled balls.

Pop the tray of balls in the freezer for 4 hours. From here, you can bag them up and they will be ready for you when you have a craving. Or after 4 hours, kick on the deep fryer or start heating the oil in a deep pot to 375°F. Also, turn the oven to 180°F. This will keep the finished balls nice and warm while you fry the others.

With a large metal slotted spoon, gently drop the balls in, careful not to crowd the pot or deep fryer. Fry till brown. Remove balls from oil and place on rack set over sheet tray to drain, and keep in warm oven till done with frying. Sprinkle balls with a bit of Kosher salt and serve.

CHEESE STICKS

A restaurant staple... just made better!

The Secret? String Cheese! Don't think restaurants are doing anything different either, except theirs are frozen and stuffed with preservatives and the crappiest cheese a few cents can buy. Hell, you can even buy a block of cheese and cut it yourself, customizing the flavor even further!

INGREDIENTS

- **1 lb. mozzarella string cheese, or a block of mozzarella cut into 3-4" blocks, about ½" thick**
- **¾ Cup all-purpose flour**
- **3 large eggs**
- **3 Tablespoons whole milk**
- **2 Cups panko or traditional breadcrumbs**

DIRECTIONS

Set up a dredging station: 1. place the flour in a shallow dish. 2. Whisk eggs and milk in a wide bowl. 3. Place breadcrumbs in another shallow dish.

Grab the mozzarella. Press it into the flour and shake off the excess. Then dunk it in the egg wash until coated, followed by pressing it into the breadcrumbs. For a thicker breading, re-dunk the coated cheese in the egg wash for a second time and press again into the breadcrumbs. Place the stick on a sheet pan. repeat till all the cheese is coated. Place sheet tray in the freezer for at least an hour.

Kick on the deep fryer or pour the oil in a deep pot and get the temperature to 375°F. Use a candy or deep-frying thermometer, and if you don't have one, GET ONE! They are a cheap investment and will make the difference between shitty deep-fried food and heavenly deep-fried food.

Working in batches as to not overcrowd the fryer or pot, fry cheese sticks for 2-3 minutes, until crispy and golden brown. Remove with a slotted spoon to paper towel lined plate to drain. Season with a sprinkling of grated parmesan and a pinch of salt.

BREADING OPTIONS

THE STANDARD BREADING IS TRADITIONAL BREAD CRUMBS. GREAT IN THEIR OWN RIGHT FOR THAT CLASSIC TEXTURE, BUT BITE CLUB IS FAR FROM TRADITIONAL. SO, LET'S HAVE SOME FUN! SWAP OUT THE BREAD CRUMBS FOR PANKO FOR A LIGHTER, AIRIER CRUST. OR THERE ARE SOME FANTASTIC FLAVORED BREAD CRUMBS BEING PRODUCED, LIKE CILANTRO LIME AND LEMON GARLIC. ADD SPICES TO THE FLOUR DREDGE.

BUT COME ON... LET'S GET CRAZY HERE. TRY PULSING SOME FLAMING HOT CHEETOS IN YOUR FOOD PROCESSOR. OR GOLDFISH CRACKERS! GOT A BAG OF PRETZEL BITS IN THE PANTRY? PULSE THEM AND ROLL THE CHEESE STICKS IN THOSE! OR TORTILLA CHIPS! OR YOUR FAVORITE POTATO CHIPS, JUST MAKE SURE TO USE THE THICK KETTLE CUT STYLE. WANT LOW CARB? USE GROUND UP PORK RINDS!

ONION RINGS

If you like it then you should eat a ring with it!

Crispy, savory, and pure umami, these rings dip wonderfully in any sauce. Perfect to top a burger with for extra crunch or serve up at a party. These fry up quick and are fully customizable! Batter these up with a traditional breadcrumb coating or plop in a deep flavored beer infused tempura.

TRADITIONAL BREADING

- **1 large sweet onion, cut into thick rings**
- **1 ½ Cups flour**
- **1 teaspoon salt**
- **1 teaspoon baking powder**
- **2 eggs, whisked**
- **½ Cup chilled club soda (plus more to thin out batter)**
- **½ Cup chilled cheap vodka (like really cheap)**
- **1 ½ Cup breadcrumbs**

Dump canola or vegetable oil (peanut oil would be the best for this) into your deep-fryer or high sided pot and rip the heat to 375°F.

Pull apart the onion into rings. In a medium bowl, pour in the flour. Press the onion rings into the flour until coated, being careful not to snap the onion. Shake off excess flour and set aside.

In the leftover flour, add the salt and baking powder and whisk to combine. Now whisk in the eggs, club soda, and vodka. You want a thin batter, so if it's too thick add more club soda. If it's really thin, add more flour.

Place a rack on a sheet pan. Dunk the onion rings into the batter until coated and set on the rack. Spread the breadcrumbs onto a plate and press the battered rings into the breadcrumbs till fully coated. You may have to scoop the breadcrumbs into the middle of the ring to coat evenly. Tap it to shake off excess breadcrumbs.

Carefully drop the rings into the hot oil and fry for 2-3 minutes until golden brown. You may have to flip the rings half way through cooking if they float.

Remove the rings to a paper towel lined plate to drain and season with a sprinkle of salt. Let cool for a bit then nosh away!

TEMPURA BEER BATTER

- **1 large sweet onion, cut into thick rings**
- **1 ½ Cups buttermilk**
- **¼ Cup cornmeal**
- **½ teaspoon chili powder**
- **1 teaspoon baking powder**
- **¾ Cup flour, plus an additional 1 Cup for dredging**
- **1 ½ teaspoons Kosher salt**
- **¼ Cup cheap vodka, chilled**
- **¾ Cup club soda, chilled**
- **¾ Cup chilled beer (lager is preferred for best taste, but stout works well too)**

Separate the onion into rings and toss into a zip top bag. Pour in buttermilk and let chill in the fridge for about an hour, giving the bag a shake half way through.

Dump the oil of choice into your deep-fryer or high sided pot and get that heat to 375°F.

In a medium bowl, whisk together the cornmeal, baking powder, chili powder, ¾ Cup flour, and salt. Keep that whisk moving and pour in the liquids. You are looking for a thin 'pancake-like' batter. Be careful not to over-mix or it will get way too dense as it sits. If it's too thick, whisk in more beer or club soda. If too thin, whisk in more flour.

In another bowl, pour in the remaining 1 Cup flour. Remove a few onion rings from the buttermilk and let excess drip off. Dredge the rings in the flour, shake off the excess, then dip into the wet batter, also letting the excess drip back into the bowl. Drop into hot oil and fry for about 2 minutes, turning rings over half way through. Batter should puff up and get perfectly crispy. Once fried, remove rings from oil and set on paper towel lined plate to drain. Season immediately with your choice of seasoning. Enjoy!

FRIED PICKLES

Whoever first said, "Hey, we should try frying pickles" should be given the frickin' Nobel Peace Prize!

Crispy, tart, and packed with savory yumminess, these were made for dunking in a rich sauce. Our go to? The Chipotle Ranch we've included on this page! Pizza sauce works great too for a pure savory combo, or a fat rich aioli. Or just sprinkle with parmesan and nosh!

INGREDIENTS

- pickle slices from a 16 oz. jar, or 4 huge deli pickles, sliced into rounds
- 1 ½ Cups flour
- ½ Cup cornstarch
- 2 teaspoons Kosher salt
- 1 ½ teaspoon ground black pepper
- ½ teaspoon chili powder
- 1 teaspoon garlic powder
- ½ teaspoon onion powder
- ½ Cup buttermilk
- 2 eggs

DIRECTIONS

Kick on your deep fryer to 375°F, or if using a thick pot, you only need to fill the oil to about an inch deep. Pour the canola or vegetable oil to 1" deep and heat to 375°F.

Drain and pat the pickles very dry. Set up your dredging stations as follows: pickles, shallow plate/bowl with ½ Cup flour, deeper bowl with buttermilk and eggs whisked together, shallow tray/plate with the remaining flour, cornstarch, salt, pepper, and spices blended together, and a lined sheet pan.

Place a few pickles into the flour, then shake off excess. Dip coated pickles into buttermilk egg wash till coated. A fork or slotted spoon makes this a lot easier and a lot less messy! Once coated in the wash, place pickles into seasoned flour mixture, pressing down gently to fully coat. If you like, you can re-dip the fully coated pickle into the wash again and re-coat in the flour for a thicker breading. But one coat is substantial for these.

In batches, place pickles in hot oil and fry for about 2 minutes. Remove from oil to a paper towel lined plate or a sheet pan with a rack set inside to drain. If making a lot, place in a 160°F oven to keep warm.

QUICKIE CHIPOTLE RANCH DIP

You've prepped enough. Let's whip this up quick so we can tear into those pickles! This is also awesome as a veggie dip!

- 1 packet dry ranch dip mix
- 2 Cups sour cream
- 4 Tablespoons fresh lime juice
- 2 Tablespoons pureed chipotle peppers
- 1 Tablespoon ground cumin
- 2 Tablespoons chopped cilantro

Toss all ingredients into a blender or food processor and blend until combined.

BEIGNETS

A New Orleans Classic with a twist!

Pillows of dough deep fried then covered with powdered sugar??? Turn up the romance by drizzling the Chocolate Red Wine Sauce (pg. 112) over them and noshing by candlelight!

INGREDIENTS

- **3/4 Cups warm water**
- **1 packet active dry yeast (or 2 ½ teaspoons)**
- **¼ Cup granulated sugar**
- **pinch Kosher salt**
- **½ Cup low fat evaporated milk**
- **1 large egg**
- **4 Cups flour**
- **2 Tablespoons vegetable shortening, cubed**

DIRECTIONS

In the bowl of your badass mixer, pour in the yeast, 1 teaspoon of sugar, and the warm water. Give a quick whisk and set aside for 10 minutes. Water should be foamy and yeast and sugars dissolved. Lock in your dough hook.

Add in the rest of the sugar, salt, evaporated milk, egg, and 2 Cups of the flour and turn the mixer on low. Dump in the shortening, then gradually add in the rest of the flour. When all ingredients are incorporated, kill the mixer and turn the dough out to a floured surface. Start kneading the dough, folding it over and over. You want a pretty firm and smooth dough. If it's still sticky, add a bit more flour.

Spray a large bowl with non-stick spray and pop the dough in. Give it a good toss to coat the ball, then cover with plastic wrap. Pop it in the fridge for 4 hours, or even better, let it sit overnight!

Now let's bang out these Beignets! First, kick the oven on to 250°F. Flip the bowl over onto a floured surface, sprinkle a bit more flour on top, and roll the dough out into a large rectangle, about 1" thick. Slice into squares. Remember these are gonna puff up when they hit the oil, so cut smaller then you think you'll want them.

Turn on the deep fryer or dump oil to about 3" deep in a heavy bottom pan and heat the oil to 350°F. Once the thermometer reads that temperature, gently lower 3-4 beignets into the oil. Since they puff, they will float, so you need to flip them about half way through, and fry for 1 ½ minutes per side. You want a golden color. Once fried, move to a paper towel lined plate/tray and pop in the oven to keep warm. When ready to serve, generously dust with powder sugar. Serve warm!

Always crack eggs on a flat surface. Cracking them on the edge of a bowl just pushes shards of shell inside the egg that you will need to fish out later...

SWEET TREATS

"I'm not a vegetarian! I'm a dessertarian!"

- Bill Watterson, from Calvin & Hobbes

"I never met a problem a proper cupcake couldn't fix."

- Sarah Ockler

OATMEAL BOURBON CHERRY COOKIES

Oatmeal cookies are often passed over... Not anymore!

Soaking dried cherries in bourbon serves two purposes. It infuses the cherries with that rich smokiness that brings a deep flavor to the cookies... AND it gives you a jar of naturally flavored cherry bourbon to craft some wonderful cocktails with!

INGREDIENTS

- 1 Cup dried cherries
- bourbon of your choice (at least ½ Cup)
- 1 ½ Cups flour
- ½ teaspoon baking powder
- ½ teaspoon salt
- ½ teaspoon baking soda
- 1 teaspoon ground cinnamon
- 1 Cup packed light brown sugar
- 2 sticks (1 Cup) butter, room temp* (see notes on next page)
- ½ Cup granulated sugar
- 2 large eggs
- 1 teaspoon vanilla extract
- 1 teaspoon almond extract
- 1 teaspoon reserved bourbon (from cherries)
- 3 Cups rolled old fashioned oats (do not use quick oats!)

DIRECTIONS

If you know you are going to make these cookies a few days before, place the cherries in a mason jar and pour in bourbon till cherries are covered. Seal jar and let sit on the counter. If these are a spur of the moment craving, place cherries in a mason jar, cover with bourbon and microwave for 1 minute. Let sit for 15 minutes before using cherries.

Rock the oven to 350°F and line a sheet tray with parchment or silicone baking mats.

In a bowl, mix flour, baking powder, salt, baking soda, and cinnamon. In the bowl of your electric mixer, cream together the brown sugar, regular sugar, and butter using the paddle attachment until nice and smooth. Crack in one egg, mix, then crack in the other. Next, dump in the extracts and 1 teaspoon of the bourbon from the jar of cherries. Now's a good time to drain the cherries. Using a strainer over a bowl, dump the cherries out. Place the bourbon back in a jar. Use this to make cocktails by adding 2 oz. of this infused bourbon to 12 oz. of cherry Dr. Pepper. CRAZY GOOD!

Once the butter/sugar/extract mixture is mixed, start adding flour mix to the bowl. After fully combined, pour in the oats, 1 Cup at a time. During the last 30 seconds of mixing, add the infused cherries.

Scoop dough on to lined sheet trays. Size is your call, but aim for at least a 1 ½" ball of dough, and make sure there is at least 2" of space between dough piles. Bake till golden brown, about 14 minutes. When the middle looks just slightly underbaked, pull them out. Let rest on sheet tray for about 10 minutes to set, then move to cooling rack. Repeat with remaining dough. Nosh, then store remaining cookies in airtight container (if there are any left).

BOURBON CHERRY BANANA BREAD

Taking the ho-hum to Fuck Yeah!

Is banana bread technically a cake? Who cares?!? Let's booze this bitch up with some infused cherries and bring this classic bakery staple to the next level!

INGREDIENTS

- 1 Cup dried cherries
- bourbon of your choice (at least ½ Cup)
- 1 stick unsalted butter, room temperature
- ½ Cup sugar
- ¼ Cup honey
- 3 very ripe large bananas
- 2 large eggs, lightly beaten
- 1 ½ Cups all-purpose flour, plus more for dusting
- ½ teaspoon salt
- 1 teaspoon baking soda
- 1 teaspoon vanilla extract
- 1 teaspoon bourbon from cherries

DIRECTIONS

Like the Bourbon Cherry Oatmeal Cookies on the previous page, if you know you are going to make this a few days before, place the cherries in a mason jar and pour in the bourbon until cherries are covered. Seal jar and let sit on the counter. If this is a spur of the moment craving, place cherries in a mason jar, cover with bourbon, and microwave for 1 minute. Let sit for 15 minutes before using cherries. When ready to use cherries, use a strainer over a bowl and dump the cherries out. Place the bourbon back in a jar for cocktails.

Kick the oven to 350° F and grease and flour a loaf pan. In the bowl of your mixer, cream the butter, sugar, and honey until smooth. Toss in the ripe bananas and mix until mashed. Add eggs and mix till blended.

In another bowl, mix flour, salt, and baking soda, then while mixer is running at medium speed, slowly pour in flour mixture to wet batter. Add in extract, bourbon, and cherries and mix for 10 seconds. Take a shot for yourself, you deserve it!

Pour batter into greased and floured loaf pan and bake for 60 minutes or until a toothpick/knife/cake tester comes out clean. Remove from oven, let rest in the pan for 10 minutes, then remove to a wire rack. Serve at room temp. Do not use as sandwich bread. Don't be that person.

FORGOT TO GET THE BUTTER TO ROOM TEMP?

SIMPLE FIX. TAKE A PINT GLASS OR MUG LARGE ENOUGH TO FIT THE STICK OF BUTTER STANDING STRAIGHT UP. PLACE THE GLASS OR MUG IN THE MICROWAVE FOR 2 MINUTES. REMOVE GLASS/MUG (CAREFUL... HOT!), STAND THE BUTTER ON ITS END AND PLACE THE GLASS/MUG OVER THE BUTTER. IN 10-15 MINUTES, THE BUTTER SHOULD BE CLOSE TO ROOM TEMPERATURE. THIS TRICK ALSO WORKS WITH EGGS AND CREAM CHEESE!

CHOCOLATE RED WINE SAUCE

Perfect dipper for fruits, breads, cakes, and fingers!

Red wine and chocolate pair so wonderfully together. If you have a small 2 Cup slow cooker, you can dump it in there to keep it warm for a party setting.

INGREDIENTS

- ¾ Cup heavy cream
- ¾ Cup red wine (sweeter the better)
- 1 ½ Tablespoons unsweetened cocoa powder
- ½ Cup sugar
- 8 oz. semi-sweet chocolate, coarsely chopped
- 4 Tablespoons unsalted butter, room temperature
- ⅛ teaspoon sea salt

DIRECTIONS

In a saucepan over medium heat, stir the cream, wine, cocoa, and sugar together. Simmer for 6 minutes, stirring every minute or so to insure no lumps form. Take the pot off the heat and stir in the butter, chocolate, and salt. Give it a taste. Add more cocoa or sugar if needed.

If you use it now, it'll be like a thin ganache. It will thicken as it cools, becoming like a frosting.

This will keep for 2 weeks in the fridge. If you need to thin it out to use it at a later time, pop it in the microwave for 15 seconds at a time and stir after each heating.

SIMPLE & RICH CHOCOLATE SAUCE

Not everything needs booze to be perfect!

This is the Swiss army knife of chocolate sauces! Top ice cream, use in chocolate milk, dip fruit in it… the uses are endless! Feel free to double or triple the recipe to fit your needs!

INGREDIENTS

- ½ Cup cold milk or heavy cream
- ½ Cup unsweetened cocoa powder
- 1 Cup sugar
- ⅛ teaspoon sea salt
- 2 teaspoons extract (vanilla, peppermint, orange, almond, etc.)

Mix all ingredients except extract in a cold sauce pan and stir to make sure there are no lumps. Place over medium-high heat and bring to just about a boil, stirring occasionally.

Once it starts to boil, reduce heat to a simmer. Now's the time to stir constantly. Simmer for 45 seconds and remove from heat. Let cool for 10 minutes, then stir in the extract.

This will thicken as it cools. Will keep in the fridge for 2 weeks. To use, reheat in the microwave in 15 second bursts until it reaches the desired consistency.

KIWI SORBET

Make something the kids will love with this frequently overlooked fuzzy fruit!

Refreshing flavor that serves as an amazing low fat dessert and a wonderful palate cleanser! If you have an ice cream maker, it really speeds up the process. But you can make this without one!

INGREDIENTS

- 18 oz. peeled and chopped ripe kiwi
- 1 ¾ oz. Caster Sugar (see notes)
- 1 ripe lime, juiced
- 7 oz. pineapple juice
- 7 oz. water

DIRECTIONS

Place the peeled and chopped kiwi in a bowl and pour the Caster Sugar over the chunks. Toss to coat and let rest 1 hour to let the sugar meld.

Place the kiwi mixture into a blender or food processor with all the juices from the bowl. Pour in lime juice, pineapple juice, and water and pulse to mix. Taste the mixture and add more Caster Sugar if not sweet enough, or add more lime juice if overly sweet.

IF YOU HAVE AN ICE CREAM MAKER: Pour the mixture into the bowl of the maker and churn until almost frozen. Dump into an air tight container, place a piece of plastic wrap over the sorbet and press down to push out as much air as possible. Place cover on and throw in freezer till frozen, at least 4-5 hours.

NO ICE CREAM MAKER: Place mixture into a freezer zip top bag, squeeze out as much air as possible, and seal. Place in freezer and get the bag to lay as flat as possible. Freeze till solid. Once solid, break into chunks and place into a food processor or super blender. Pulse until smooth. You can also throw in any mix-ins at this time to blend them in.

MAKE YOUR OWN CASTER SUGAR!!!

ACTUAL CASTER SUGAR IS SOMETIMES VERY HARD TO FIND AT LOCAL GROCERY STORES. EVEN MY OWN CHOICE STORES DO NOT CARRY IT. BUT IT'S EASY TO MAKE YOURSELF!

CASTER SUGAR IS JUST PLAIN OLD SUGAR. IT'S FINER THEN GRANULATED SUGAR, BUT NOT AS FINE AS POWDERED SUGAR.

PUT SUGAR INTO A COFFEE GRINDER (BEST METHOD), HIGH SPEED BLENDER, OR FOOD PROCESSOR (ENOUGH SUGAR TO COVER THE BLADES, SO IT MAY BE A LOT MORE THEN 1 CUP). PULSE IN BURSTS OF ABOUT 5-6 SECONDS EACH UNTIL FINE GRANULES REMAIN.

BAKED DOUGHNUTS

Skip the previously frozen stuff from the chains!

CHOCOLATE

- 1 large egg
- ½ Cup granulated sugar
- ⅓ Cup milk
- ¼ Cup plain yogurt
- 2 Tablespoons unsalted butter, melted
- ½ teaspoon vanilla extract
- 1 Cup flour
- ½ teaspoon baking soda
- ⅛ teaspoon salt
- ½ teaspoon baking powder
- ¼ Cup unsweetened cocoa powder

Glaze Parings:

• Classic • Chocolate • Vanilla • Peanut Butter •
• Cream Cheese • Cherry •

DIRECTIONS

Rock the oven to 350°F. Give a donut pan a quick spritz with nonstick spray.

In the bowl of your mixer with the whisk attachment, blend the egg, sugar, milk, yogurt, melted butter, and extract until combined.

In another bowl, stir together the flour, baking soda, salt, baking powder, and cocoa. Once mixed, turn on mixer and add flour mixture to the wet batter and mix it till just combined. Batter should be thick.

Pour the batter into a piping bag, zip top bag, or just use a spoon. Fill the donut cavities ¾ of the way full.

Bake for 10 minutes. Start testing the donuts at 8 minutes by poking with a toothpick. Comes out clean, donuts are ready. Allow to rest in the pan for 10 minutes before removing to a rack to cool for glazing and noshing.

VANILLA

- 1 Cup flour
- 1 teaspoon baking powder
- ⅓ Cup sugar
- ½ teaspoon salt
- 1 egg
- 7 Tablespoons milk
- 2 Tablespoons unsalted butter, melted
- 1 Tablespoon vanilla extract

DIRECTIONS

Oven to 350°F. Spray donut pan.

Whisk the dry ingredients until combined.

In a separate bowl, whisk the wet ingredients.

Mix the wet ingredients into the dry till well combined. Careful you do not over-mix. You'll end up with dense donuts.

Pipe or spoon batter into donut pan, filling ¾ of each cavity.

Bake 10 minutes or until a toothpick comes out clean. Let rest for 5 minutes in pan, then transfer to wire rack to cool. Glaze when cool.

Glaze Parings:

• Classic • Chocolate • Vanilla • Cream Cheese • Cherry • Lemon • Strawberry • Bourbon • Maple •

MORE BAKED DOUGHNUTS

PUMPKIN

- 1 Cup flour
- 1 teaspoon baking powder
- ¼ teaspoon ground nutmeg
- 1 teaspoon pumpkin pie spice
- ¼ teaspoon salt
- ⅓ Cup light brown sugar
- 1 egg, room temperature
- ¼ Cup milk
- ⅓ Cup pumpkin puree
- 3 Tablespoons unsalted butter, melted
- 1 Tablespoon vanilla extract

DIRECTIONS

Oven to 350°F. Spray donut pan.

In one bowl, mix the dry ingredients.

In another, mix the wet.

Add the dry to the wet while mixing.

Pipe or spoon the batter into donut cavities.

Bake 12 minutes or until toothpick comes out clean. Cool in pan for 5 minutes. Remove to wire rack. Cool completely. Glaze and nosh!

GLAZE PARINGS:

• Classic • Vanilla • Cream Cheese •
• Cinnamon Sugar • Maple •

There is a MASSIVE difference between Baking SODA and Baking POWDER. They are NOT swappable! Read ingredients _carefully_ and make sure you are using the correct one. They look almost identical!

LEMON

- 1 Cup all-purpose flour
- 1 teaspoon baking powder
- ½ teaspoon salt
- ¼ teaspoon baking soda
- 2 Tablespoons unsalted butter, melted
- 1 egg, room temperature
- ⅓ Cup sugar
- ¼ Cup sour cream
- ¼ Cup milk
- 1 Tablespoon vanilla extract
- 1 Tablespoon fresh lemon juice
- 1 Tablespoon lemon zest

DIRECTIONS

Oven to 350°F. Spray donut pan.

In one bowl, mix the flour, baking powder, salt, and baking soda.

In another, mix everything else.

Add the dry to the wet while mixing.

Pipe or spoon the batter into donut cavities.

Bake 10 minutes or until toothpick comes out clean. Cool in pan for 5 minutes. Remove to wire rack. Cool completely. Glaze with your faves!!

GLAZE PARINGS:

• Classic • Strawberry • Vanilla • Cream Cheese •
• Cherry • Lemon •

BAKED DOUGHNUTS

APPLE CIDER

- 1 ¾ Cups all-purpose flour
- 1 ¼ teaspoons baking powder
- 1 teaspoons ground cinnamon
- ½ teaspoon nutmeg
- ¾ teaspoon fine sea salt
- 10 Tablespoons butter (1 stick plus 2 Tablespoons), room temperature
- 1 Cup light brown sugar
- 2 Tablespoons granulated sugar
- 2 large eggs, room temperature
- 2 teaspoons vanilla extract
- ½ Cup apple cider

DIRECTIONS

Oven to 350°F. Spray donut pan.

In one bowl, mix the flour, baking powder, cinnamon, nutmeg, and salt.

In the bowl of your mixer, cream butter with the sugars until smooth. Mix in eggs, one at a time. Add in the extract.

Add the dry to the wet while mixing. Then slowly stream in apple cider while mixing till everything is well incorporated.

Pipe or spoon the batter into donut cavities.

Bake 13-15 minutes or until toothpick comes out clean. Cool in pan for 5 minutes. Remove to wire rack. Cool completely. Glaze these bitches up!!!

GLAZE PARINGS:

• Classic • Vanilla • Maple • Maple Cinnamon • Cinnamon Sugar • Bourbon • Caramel •

RED VELVET

- 1 Cup all-purpose flour
- 1 ½ teaspoon baking powder
- 2 Tablespoons unsweetened cocoa powder
- 1 teaspoon espresso powder
- ½ teaspoon salt
- ¾ Cup brown sugar
- ½ Cup buttermilk
- 3 Tablespoons butter, melted
- 1 large egg, room temperature
- 1 Tablespoon vanilla extract
- 4-5 drops red food coloring

DIRECTIONS

Oven to 350°F. Spray donut pan.

In one bowl, mix the flour, baking powder, cocoa, salt, espresso powder, and brown sugar.

In another bowl, blend the buttermilk, butter, egg, and extract.

Fold the wet into the dry. As it's mixing, add the food coloring till you achieve the desired color. If you are colorblind like me, get someone to tell you when to stop. 28 drops are WAY too many.

Pipe or spoon the batter into donut cavities.

Bake 10 minutes or until toothpick comes out clean. Cool in pan for 5 minutes. Remove to wire rack. Cool completely. Get those glazes ready!

GLAZE PARINGS:

• Classic • Vanilla • Chocolate • Cherry •

GLAZES, SPRINKLES, & UNICORN FARTS

CLASSIC DONUT SHOP GLAZE:

2 Cups powdered sugar, sifted

5 Tablespoons half & half

1 teaspoon vanilla extract

-Blend till smooth. Dip donuts and allow glaze to harden-

VANILLA GLAZE:

1 ½ Cups powdered sugar, sifted

2-3 Tablespoons milk

1 ½ teaspoons vanilla extract

-Blend all ingredients till smooth-

CHOCOLATE GLAZE:

1 ½ Cups powdered sugar, sifted

4 Tablespoons unsweetened cocoa powder

3 Tablespoons milk

1 teaspoon pure vanilla extract

-Blend all ingredients till smooth-

STRAWBERRY GLAZE:

½ Cup fresh strawberries, puree'd

1-2 Cups powdered sugar, sifted

1-2 Tablespoons cream or milk

-Press puree'd strawberries through a fine mess strainer. Mix other ingredients with the strawberry juice till smooth-

CREAM CHEESE GLAZE:

3 oz. cream cheese, soft, room temp

3 Tablespoons unsalted butter, room temp

1 teaspoon vanilla extract

2 Cups powdered sugar, sifted

-Blend all ingredients till smooth-

PEANUT BUTTER GLAZE:

1 Cup powdered sugar, sifted

2 Tablespoons creamy peanut butter

2 – 3 Tablespoons milk

⅛ teaspoon fine sea salt

-Blend all ingredients till smooth-

CINNAMON SUGAR:

1 Cup sugar

2 Tablespoons cinnamon

-Stir or shake together till blended-

TOO THICK: Add more of the liquids

TOO THIN: Add more powdered sugar

CHERRY GLAZE:

2 Cups powdered sugar, sifted

2 Tablespoons maraschino cherry syrup

1 Tablespoon amaretto liqueur

1 Tablespoon heavy cream, plus more if needed

⅛ teaspoon fine sea salt

-Blend all ingredients till smooth-

MAPLE GLAZE:

1 ½ Cups powdered sugar, sifted

2 Tablespoons milk

4 Tablespoons maple syrup

1 ½ teaspoons vanilla extract

-Blend all ingredients till smooth-

MAPLE CINNAMON GLAZE:

1 Cup powdered sugar, sifted

½ teaspoon ground cinnamon

1 Tablespoon pure maple syrup

1 Tablespoon milk, or more as needed

-Blend all ingredients till smooth-

BOURBON GLAZE:

1 ½ Cups powdered sugar, sifted

1 Tablespoon honey

3 Tablespoons bourbon

1 Tablespoon lemon juice

-Blend all ingredients till smooth-

LEMON GLAZE:

½ Cup freshly squeezed lemon juice

2 Cups powdered sugar, sifted

1 Tablespoon unsalted butter, melted

1 lemon, zest finely grated

-Blend all ingredients till smooth-

CARAMEL GLAZE:

1 (14 oz.) can sweetened condensed milk

1 Cup light brown sugar

2 Tablespoons butter, melted

½ teaspoon vanilla extract

⅛ teaspoon fine sea salt

-Combine milk and sugar in a pot and bring to a simmer over medium heat. Reduce to low and cook, stirring constantly for 5 minutes. Remove from the heat and stir in rest of ingredients-

BOURBON CARAMEL SAUCE

Another Bourbon recipe? I may have a problem...

I developed this caramel sauce to top a succulent bread pudding *cough cough... next page... cough*. For a twist, feel free to use flavored bourbons. Cherry and cinnamon work very well and the new lines of peanut butter bourbons will add an amazing twist of flavor!

INGREDIENTS

- 1 Cup white sugar
- 1 Cup packed brown sugar (light or dark)
- ½ Cup water
- 1 Cup heavy cream (warmed)
- 1 Tablespoon light corn syrup
- ½ Cup bourbon
- ½ teaspoon fine sea salt

DIRECTIONS

In a medium saucepan bring the sugar, water, and corn syrup to a boil over high heat. Cook until the sugar is dissolved, washing down the side of the pan with a wet pastry brush. Continue cooking without stirring, until an amber caramel forms, about 6 minutes. Remove from the heat and carefully stir in the cream. Let cool for 1 minute, then stir in the bourbon. Bring the mixture to a boil over moderate heat and cook, stirring for 1 minute. Let the caramel sauce cool slightly and serve warm or at room temperature. This will keep in a fridge for up to 2 weeks. Warm to use.

WET VS. DRY METHODS

THERE ARE 2 WAYS TO MAKE CARAMEL SAUCE. THE WET METHOD USES WATER TO AID IN THE MELTING OF SUGAR. THIS METHOD IS EASIER IN PREVENTING THE SUGARS FROM BURNING, BUT TAKES LONGER BECAUSE YOU HAVE TO WAIT TO EVAPORATE THE WATER FULLY BEFORE THE SUGARS START TO CARAMELIZE. PLUS, YOU HAVE TO BRUSH DOWN THE SIDES OF THE POT TO KEEP THE SUGARS FROM CRYSTALLIZING.

THE DRY METHOD USES STRAIGHT HEAT TO MELT THE SUGARS SLOWLY. INSTEAD OF MELTING THE SUGARS ALL AT ONCE, YOU MELT THE SUGARS A LITTLE AT A TIME. THIS METHOD ALLOWS YOU TO CONTROL THE COLOR AND DEPTH OF FLAVOR OF THE CARAMEL SAUCE.

Scientifically, alcohol evaporates at 172°F within 30 seconds. Realistically, it all depends on the vessel. Wide pan and shallow depth, sure. Narrow pot filled with a stew like thick food will take longer to evaporate all the alcohol. Rule of thumb: Just because you hit 172°F for 30 seconds, don't assume the dish is completely alcohol free.

BREAD PUDDING

Three different breads, 1 freaking amazing treat!

The breads here (brioche, croissant, and challah) combine to make a savory, melt in your mouth dessert. Top it with a hearty pour of our warmed Bourbon Caramel Sauce and win the pot luck!!!

INGREDIENTS

- ½ stick unsalted butter
- 4 Cups milk
- 1 teaspoon salt
- ⅔ Cup sugar
- 1 Tablespoon vanilla extract
- 1 lb. combination of brioche, croissant, and challah bread (or see notes below for more options)
- 1 Cup dried cherries (optional)
- 4 eggs, beaten

DIRECTIONS

In a saucepan, melt butter over low heat. Once melted, stir in the milk, salt, sugar, and vanilla. Continue to cook and stir until sugar is dissolved. Remove from the heat and let cool. While the mixture cools, cut all of the breads into 2" cubes, mix in the dried cherries and place into a 9" X 13" baking dish.

Once mixture has cooled, stir in beaten eggs and whisk till combined. Pour mix over cubed bread and let sit for at least an hour.

While the bread is soaking in the goodness, kick the oven on to 350°F.

After an hour, toss that bad boy into the oven and bake for 30 to 45 minutes. You want the mixture you poured in (technically it's a custard of sorts at this point) to be set, but still have a bit of wobble to it if the pan is shaken. You also want the edges of the bread sticking out of the custard to be a bit brown.

Remove from oven and serve warm. This can also be served sitting at room temperature. Now's the time to pour over that Bourbon Caramel Sauce!!! You made it, right???? RIGHT???

LAST BUT NOT YEAST....

THE CHOICES FOR THE BREAD ARE INFINITE FOR BREAD PUDDING. YOU CAN LITERALLY JUST MAKE THIS OUT OF SLICES OF WHITE BREAD, BUT IT WON'T BE AS GOOD. I USE THOSE 3 BREADS (ABOVE) BECAUSE THEY ARE TYPICALLY COMPOSED FROM A HIGHER FAT DOUGH, WHICH LEAVES A SILKY, RICH BREAD PUDDING.

MIX IT UP! MAKE IT FROM FRENCH BREAD! OR SWAP THE CHALLAH WITH A RICH CHOCOLATE SWIRL BREAD. USE FLAVORED CROISSANTS. TOSS IN SOME SOURDOUGH, BAGELS, HAMBURGER BUNS, HAWAIIAN ROLLS... GO NUTS! DISCOVER FLAVORS! THAT GOES FOR THE "ADD-INS" AS WELL! SWAP THE CHERRIES FOR RAISINS OR OTHER DRIED FRUIT. TOSS IN CINNAMON, NUTMEG, OR EVEN PUMPKIN PIE SPICE.

WHIP CREAM - 3 WAYS

That crap from a tub is literally just whipped lard

PLAIN

- 1 Cup COLD heavy whipping cream
- ¼ Cup powdered sugar
- 1-2 teaspoons vanilla extract

CHOCOLATE

PLAIN WHIP CREAM RECIPE +

- ¼ Cup unsweetened cocoa powder

BOOZY

PLAIN WHIP CREAM RECIPE +

- ¼ Cup Irish cream liqueur OR
- 1 ½ Tablespoons dark rum OR
- 1 ½ Tablespoons bourbon (plain or flavored) OR
- ¼ Cup Bailey's OR
- 2 Tablespoons flavored vodka

OR ANY OTHER ALCOHOL!!! Start with 1 Tablespoon of the booze (or 2 Tablespoons if it's a cream liqueur) and add it as the cream whips. Taste test as it whips and add more if needed.

NOTE: ADDING BOOZE TO WHIP CREAM KEEPS IT FULL PROOF, SO PROBABLY NOT THE BEST TO SERVE IT FOR THE KIDDO'S BIRTHDAY.

DIRECTIONS

Let's go with the best, easiest, and most consistent way to make whip cream... the stand mixer (or hand mixer).

Place the bowl and whisk of mixer in the fridge for at least 30 minutes. Remove from fridge, lock into the mixer, and add all ingredients.

Start on low speed and increase to a high speed as it firms up. Make sure to stop at least once to scrape down the sides of the bowl. Keep mixing till stiff peaks form. Serve or place in piping bag or just dunk head in it.

FOR CHOCOLATE:

Add in the chocolate. Start with 2 Tablespoons and increase to your desired taste. If you go with at least ¼ Cup, you may have to increase the powdered sugar, Tablespoon at a time.

CONSISTENCY CHART:

THE PLOP: Looks like runny ice cream. No good, keep whipping.

SOFT PEAKS: Peaks fall over on whisk. Looks like stirred yogurt. Super silky. Keep going.

MEDIUM PEAKS: Tips of peaks slowly fall over but hold their shape on the whisk. Most common consistency and is used for cake layers, frostings, pie topping, or fillings in pastries.

STIFF PEAKS: Peaks hold their shape on the whisk. This is the thickness you want for folding into cheesecakes or for cakes. Perfect consistency for trifles as it will stand up to fruits and fillings.

OVER WHIPPED (CURDLED): Lumpy and clumps that look like cheap shaving cream. It's ruined. It cannot be saved at this point, but why waste good cream? If you keep whipping it at this point, you'll make an oddly (or possibly delicious) flavored churned butter.

WHIP IT GOOD!

Whip it, shake it or charge it! Either way, it's time to get creamy!

You don't need to rely on the tubs of what is basically whipped lard or cans of compressed air and scientific ingredients to have whip cream. Make it yourself and you will never go back to that store-bought crap. It's so customizable, and man, the flavor just can't be beat (pun totally intended)! From shaking to a nitro based whip cream charger, fresh whip cream is literally just minutes in the making.

SHAKER METHOD

The bare bones of methods, all it takes is a mason jar or shaker bottle. Place all ingredients in the jar or bottle, seal, and shake shake shake!

HAND WHIPPING METHOD

Strap on the fitness band and get ready for the best arm workout you can get in the kitchen! Chill your bowl and whisk for at least 15 minutes, then dump in the ingredients and start whipping. This method will give you the best control over the peaks of the cream and it's kinda fun to watch the transformation from liquid to semi-solid, but you are going to be too exhausted to enjoy it. I *do not* recommend this method.

MIXER METHOD

Use the whisk attachment and start on medium low speed as you mix the ingredients. Once the mixture gets foamy, kick the speed up to medium-high until soft peaks form. Then lower the speed slightly to create medium or stiff peaks. But be careful, at this point it can go from perfection to curdled mess.

BLENDER METHOD

Probably the quickest way to make whip cream, this pulls it together in about 20 seconds. Pop the ingredients in and start on the lowest speed to blend the ingredients, then kick it to the highest speed to add in the air. This will only take 10-20 seconds, and it helps to do it in 5 second bursts to make sure you don't overdo it. Scrape down the sides of the blender to make sure everything is getting mixed properly.

FOOD PROCESSOR METHOD

Similar to the blender method, because of the bowl size, the whip cream comes together in just under a minute. Start slow till ingredients are mixed, then kick it into overdrive!

CHARGER METHOD
(ALSO KNOWN AS A WHIP CREAM DISPENSER)

Pour the ingredients in, fasten the top down tightly, and screw in a nitrogen cartridge till you hear a hiss (larger containers will require two charges). Shake the canister 6-12 times, turn over, and dispense!

Adult Fun Time Drinkies

These are just some fun and crazy delicious drinks we like to throw together for no reason other than to enjoy and have fun with our dinner parties. Some are spin-offs of drinks recreated from theme bars, some are hybrids.... but all are soooo goooooooodddddddddd!

LEMONGRASSASSIN

Rum-arkable taste like a shot to the Coco-nuts!

The star of the show is the hand-crafted lemongrass syrup, which is incredibly easy to make. But be careful... this bad boy goes down smooth and will knock you on your Lemongrass fast!

INGREDIENTS

- **5 oz. coconut rum**
- **3 oz. fresh Lemongrass Syrup (recipe below)**
- **1 ½ oz. freshly squeezed lime juice**

FOR THE LEMONGRASS SIMPLE SYRUP:

- **3-4 stalks fresh lemongrass, washed, and coarsely chopped (keep 1-2 stalks on hand for bottling)**
- **2 Cups water**
- **1 ½ Cup sugar**

DIRECTIONS

Start by making the lemongrass simple syrup. We got to let it cool down before using, so aim to make about 4 hours prior to pouring. Pop the lemongrass, water, and sugar into a pot and bring to a boil. Stir constantly to dissolve the sugar. Once boiling, lower heat to low, offset a lid on the pot and simmer for 15 minutes. While this is simmering, grab something to put the syrup into, like a glass bar bottle or a mason jar. Wash and sanitize by rinsing all soap from the container (don't dry it) then microwaving for 4 minutes. Leave the glass in the micro until ready to use. Be warned, it will be very hot so handle accordingly. Once simmered, strain the syrup into the sanitized bottle/jar. Add the remaining stalks of lemongrass and stash in the fridge to chill the hell out.

Ready to make the drink? Grab a cocktail shaker, tall mason jar, pitcher... whatever. Fill it with ice, add drink ingredients, and shake/stir for 10 seconds. Strain into glasses. Enjoy!

CRAFTING SIMPLE SYRUPS

1 Cup Sugar + 1 Cup Water + Desired Flavors

Bring water and sugar to a gentle boil. Still until sugar is dissolved. Add in flavors. Simmer 5 minutes. Remove from heat and allow to cool. Strain before bottling.

For a thicker, sweeter syrup: 2 Cups sugar + 1 Cup water • For a thinner syrup: 1 Cup sugar + 2 Cups water

Simple syrups have so many uses, from flavoring cocktails, teas, and coffees, to soaking cakes, to even acting as a quick glaze for meats and veggies! Snow cone flavors? Just simple syrups! What's awesome is that you can almost use ANYTHING to make a flavored syrup. Basics include a vanilla bean or a spoonful of lavender, to a handful of mint or rosemary, to a cup of fruit. Flowers, candies, booze, and veggies (if you want to go that route)! You can even cheat and use extracts if you wish! Want low cal simple syrups? Just swap the sugar with the sugar substitute of your choice (it will be thinner than standard simple syrup, but can be thickened up with ½ teaspoon of xanthan gum) at a 1:1 ratio. You can even use brown sugar to get a more molasses packed syrup (use as a substitution for maple syrup). Play with the amounts of desired flavors until you achieve the potency you like!

JOHNNY D'S ICED WEEEEEEEEEE

The ultimate summer guzzler!

A John Daley is when you add alcohol to an Arnold Palmer. This version swaps out the vodka for a smooth peach bourbon that blends so perfectly into the tea and lemonade combo that you'll be 3 glasses in before you realize you should've stopped after the first!

INGREDIENTS

- packet of iced tea mix (enough to make 2 qts.)
- packet of lemonade mix (enough to make 2 qts.)
- 750 ml. bottle of Evan Willams Peach Bourbon
- fresh or canned peach slices
- mint leaves (optional)

DIRECTIONS

12 hours before making, place the drained canned peaches or fresh sliced peaches in the freezer.

When ready to make, grab a container that can hold at least a gallon and a half. Fill container with a gallon of cold water and dump the iced tea and lemonade powders. Stir until fully dissolved. Next, dump the entire bottle of peach bourbon in and stir. Remove peach slices from freezer and place into container or use them as an alternative to ice in glasses. Stir in mint leaves if desired, or leave them out for individual glasses. Serve.

SECRET OF THE OOZE

This will definitely turn you into something!

Cowabunga dudes and dudettes!

INGREDIENTS

- 1½ oz. Smirnoff green apple vodka
- 2 oz. Sour Apple Pucker
- 2 oz. Hawaiian Punch Green Berry Rush
- lime slices (optional)

DIRECTIONS

Place ice into a cocktail shaker and pour ingredients in. Give a few good shakes and strain into rocks or martini glasses. Add lime slice if so inclined. Pairs well with pizza... but then again, what doesn't.

If you can't find Green Berry Rush, you can use any green punch. It's more for color then taste, as the alcohol will take over the flavor profile. Hell, even Mountain Dew will work in a pinch.

BRAKE FLUID

This one will stop you in your tracks!

Don't let the ingredients or the viscosity throw you off. This one is crazy smooth. Need to make a huge batch? It's totally scalable!

INGREDIENTS

- 1 part Southern Comfort
- 1 part orange juice
- 1 part amaretto
- 1 part Mountain Dew
- 1 part maraschino juice or grenadine
- 1 part vodka

DIRECTIONS

Throw all into a shaker, mason jar, bowl, oil pan… whatever! Shake or stir till combined. Serve over ice or chilled as a shot.

ANTI-FREEZE

We got Brake Fluid… so why not?

For a thicker consistency, you can toss the vodka and Midori in the freezer for a few hours before making. Careful scaling this cause it's really potent.

INGREDIENTS

- 2 parts Sprite (Zero is ok as well)
- 2 parts citrus vodka (I recommend Absolut Citron)
- 1 part Midori Melon
- ice

DIRECTIONS

Dump everything into a shaker glass over ice. Give 1 or 2 shakes, just enough to work the Sprite up. Strain into shot glasses.

GIMME S'MORE FIREBALL!

Let's Get Toasted!

Let's bring the classic campfire classic to a rocks glass near you!

INGREDIENTS

- 5 graham crackers, crushed to all hell
- marshmallow crème, spread on a plate
- 2 oz. Fireball (or other cinnamon whisky)
- 2 oz. vanilla schnapps
- 4 oz. chocolate liqueur

DIRECTIONS

Grab your favorite rocks, shot, or martini glass and dip the rim into the marshmallow crème, coating the rim completely. If you want to be fancy AF, toast some marshmallows over the stove or fire, then run them along the rim. This may get messy. Embrace it.

Dump the crushed graham crackers onto a shallow plate and dip the rim of the glass into it.

Measure out the boozy parts into a shaker, add some ice, and give it a heavy shake or two. Strain into the rimmed glass. Grab a seat by the fire and enjoy.

Big Papa Pepper

If you love Big Red gum, your gonna love this drink!

This very simple drink is often made for parties, and is so delicious and easy to throw together. Also, it can be scaled wonderfully.

INGREDIENTS

- 3 parts plain or Cherry Dr. Pepper (diet, too!)
- 1 part Fireball or other cinnamon whiskey
- 1 sweet cherry per glass
- ice

DIRECTIONS

Take a straw and drive it through the top of the cherry to push the seed out. Leave the cherry on the bottom of the straw. Add ingredients in this order: ice, Fireball, Dr. Pepper. The cherry will soften a bit as it takes on the acid of the soda, giving it a soft but flavor packed finish when you nosh it at the end of the drink.

129

Flash (orange) and Methos (gray). These guys were always interested in what I was cooking, and I always let them taste test. Flash used to sit on a stool as I cooked and I would explain what I was doing. He helped me work out a lot of culinary problems, and always kept me calm when I started getting crazy. Methos passed in 2010, Flash in 2017. These two made me the "cat guy" I am today.

I miss these guys like crazy.

The Noodle Guru Mr. J (L), Skully (R), and the newest nutjob Damascus (top, with the little devil horns). Mr. J was adopted from animal control as a kitten, as he chose me by sitting in my lap. Skully and Damascus were rescued Feral's. These guys are beyond loving and amazing in their own ways.

Just some of my favorite picts of Mr. J and I.

And although I love all my kitties equally, Mr. J has become my buddy, my right paw man. My Noodle Guru for life.

BITECLUBNOMS.com

BITE
BAKEHOUSE
CLUB

BITE CLUB

BITE CLUB

BITE
CLUB
DAME

The BC Dames Official Logo

Nothing like having a group of strong, independent, and amazing women in your life.

This amazing piece was created by Tabitha of Sea Cosy on Etsy. Painted on a real surfboard fin, she was one of the first guests (and my very first international guest) to attend my Bite Club Dinner Parties.

This was my first public convention after creating Bite Club. I was given a table at the Galaxy Comic Book & Fantasy Art Expo, totally unsure how a jerky vendor would do in this environment. I was surrounded by some of the coolest artists and cosplayers... I was just a chef.

I had 75 bags of our jerky across 8 flavors. I was sure I would be returning with at least ¾ of those.

I couldn't have been more wrong.

I sold out in the first 4 hours, with many coming back to the table for more; only to see "SOLD OUT" in black letters on the table. I was taking digital orders at that point. Many of the artists themselves were upset because they saw people coming up to their tables with bags of my jerky, but were unable to get up themselves to procure some.

After the event, even the organizer admitted he wasn't sure how well I would fair... but because people kept talking about Bite Club throughout the day to him... I had no choice. I was returning the next year. I laughed and fully accepted those terms.

The next year I doubled my inventory to 150 bags of jerky. I sold 1/4th of the stock to the artists themselves before the doors even opened... each one saying "I wasn't taking any chances this year!" I still sold out in 4 hours.

But the biggest moment was when I had guests coming to me as soon as doors opened. Fans of Bite Club. They came for my goods, and to meet me.

I... I had fans...

I've been floating ever since...

Welp, this is what gets the "Parental Advisory" sticker on the cover.

Look at that melon of a head!

Sorry mom...

3 months

CHEF TONY
00

"Sometimes your biggest fans are the smallest ones."

My Nephew Gage. Or as his chef jacket says... "12-Gage"

Hells yeah, I have the coveted Golden Weiner Trophy for winning the "Wurst Chef in Will County" Brat Cookoff in 2022! I kissed it like I had won the Stanley Cup when I received it.

Our sticker was spotted stuck to a support inside the Oxford University Museum of Natural History in the UK!!!

Bite Club is officially International!

(We do not promote vandalizing historic structures with our swag.)

This was an accidental snap during a photoshoot. What was an oopsie turned out to be such a meaningful photo to me. It was taken during a major transformation in my life, where I was shedding the toxicity of my past life and really coming into my own with self confidence, not only personally, but within my culinary future as well. I see this photo as my "rebirth" shot. Chef Tony 2.0!!!

"A NEW CHALLENGER ENTERS THE ARENA"

I have absolutely no problem laughing at myself. I'm a kid at heart.

I will always be proud of what I built.

If it all fails today, then tomorrow I will learn and grow. I will rebuild and excel.

Two of the biggest supporters in my life... Mom and Sous Chef Heather. The exhaustion in my face shows the 2 months of development hell I went through to win the cookoff.

Totally worth it!

I was tasked to create a speciality drink for a Halloween party at a museum fundraiser. I called it "Bad Moon Rising". This was taken as a final test run to make sure the viscosity of the top layer of the drink held up.

IMAGE BY JAY FOSGITT

IMAGE BY JOE SPICER

IMAGE BY JASON ESSEX

CHEF PROFILE

Tony C. is the Owner and Executive Chef at Bite Club, which he prides in making small batch, hand-crafted, made to order noms. He has been featured in numerous food based magazines and podcasts, and in 2017, he was named "Foodie to Follow" by Sprialized Magazine. In 2022, he took home the coveted "Wurst Chef in Will County" award for his custom-made brats. Tony grew up in Chicago most of his life, only recently relocating to Indiana to expand Bite Club to its full potential. He has written specialized spec menus for numerous businesses and 501c3s for fund raising efforts, and has a killer knack for coming up with creative names for foods and executing them to full perfection. He specializes in elevating comfort foods and keeping a realistic approach to his culinary madness so anyone can easily follow his recipes using the tools and ingredients they probably already have in their kitchen. His love for his kitties can be seen on his social media feeds, as well as through his work with local cat rescues. Plans to open a communal kitchen where chefs, bakers, and foodies can teach, learn, and grow their passion or business are in the works, as well as opening a Bite Club themed food truck.